Jake Gaither
America's Most Famous Black Coach

"The most famous black coach in America is Jake Gaither, head football coach and athletic director at Florida A&M."

—*Sports Illustrated*
Sept. 8, 1969

Jake Gaither
America's Most Famous Black Coach

by George E. Curry
ILLUSTRATED WITH PHOTOGRAPHS AND DIAGRAMS

DODD, MEAD & COMPANY, NEW YORK

1 2 3 4 5 6 7 8 9 10

Library of Congress Cataloging in Publication Data

Curry, George E
  Jake Gaither, America's most famous Black coach.

    1. Gaither, Alonzo S. 2. Football coaches—United
States—Biography. I. Title.
GV939.G3C87   796.33'2'0924 [B]   76–50580
ISBN 0–396–07381–6

For Jackie and my parents,
William and Martha Polk

Acknowledgments

It is impossible to acknowledge within this limited space all the persons who have been helpful in the preparation of this book. I thank all those who are unnamed herein as well as all those who told me they couldn't wait until I finished the book; of course, they lied.

Some individuals, particularly those still on the staff at Florida A&M, have requested anonymity; a few persons who made only marginal contributions asked that I record their names for posterity. Members of both groups—fortunately for some and unfortunately for the others—shall remain nameless.

I would be remiss if I failed to publicly express my appreciation to the individuals who graciously assisted me in this endeavor. Among them: Bill McGrotha of the *Tallahassee Democrat;* Glen Kirchhoff of the *Miami Herald;* Carl Nesfield of *Black Sports* magazine; Carl E. Morris, editor of *The New Pittsburgh Courier,* Henrietta Grant, former dean of admissions at Knoxville College; Cordell Thompson of *Jet;* Mrs. Louise M. Rountree, assistant librarian at Livingstone College; Hansel E. Tookes, athletic director of Florida A&M; Rita Montgomery; William R. Henderson; Bob Shay; Ernest L. Fillyau, FAMU's official photographer; and four friends who alternately needled and encouraged me, mostly the former, until I finished the book—William E. Owens, Ralph M. Ross, Gerald M. Boyd and Joseph DePasquale.

Special thanks are due Roosevelt Wilson, Florida A&M's superb sports information director and, of course, Sadie and Jake Gaither.

I wish to express my appreciation to *Post-Dispatch* Managing Editor Evarts A. Graham, Jr., Assistant Managing Editor Dave Lipman, and Executive City Editor Charlie Prendergast for their encouragement and permitting me to alter my work schedule, not to mention habits.

A number of my former colleagues at *Sports Illustrated* were particularly encouraging: Ron Scott, who has since defected to *People;* Jim Kaplan, Don Delliquanti, Myra Gelband, Kent Hannon, Stephanie Salter, Larry Keith, Merv Hyman, Jerry Tax, Andy Crichton, Bob Creamer, Tex Maule, and Mort Sharnick.

I wish to express my gratitude to my wife, Jackie, for her love, tolerance, understanding and encouragement; I accept the responsibility for the fact that she has since begun talking to plants.

My sisters—Charlotte, Chris, and Sue—and my parents provided me with enough love and confidence to sustain me throughout my life, including the writing of this book.

I would like to thank Henry Holbert and Lou Mims, my football coaches at Druid High School, and I. G. Brown, my coach at Knoxville College, for all they taught me about football and the time they wasted trying to make me a quarterback. It was not all in vain, however, because when Jake Gaither mentioned split ends, I knew he was not talking about hair. I also thank Mrs. Hazel Hackett, Mc Donald Hughes, Robert L. Glynn, Carl R. Baldwin and Robert L. Owens III, all of whom have been especially inspirational.

Finally, I would like to list all my aunts, uncles, and cousins, but there are just too many of them. I love them, anyway.

GEORGE E. CURRY

St. Louis, Missouri

Contents

Jake Gaither
America's Most Famous Black Coach

1

Hubba, Hubba

On December 5, 1959, Florida A&M University was preparing to play Prairie View College in Miami for the National Collegiate Black Championship. Both teams were unbeaten at the time. To the tune of the Afro-American sprirual "Nothing But the Righteous," the A&M players sang, "Nothing but the Rattlers, yes I do . . . louder now. Nothin' but the Rattlers. Sing it children. . . ." Ten minutes before kickoff, Jake Gaither strolled into the dressing room under the north stands.

"I'm not going to kid anybody," Gaither said, pausing for effect. "I'm scared to death." Another pause. "I like to feel this way, though. It feels good until the whistle blows. And tonight we're playing for the championship."

The team shouted a symphonic, "Hubba, Hubba!"

Gaither continued. "You've played good ball this year. You've come from behind."

"Hubba, Hubba," seconded the Rattlers.

"You boys have been playing sixty-minute football. Now, we can't afford to make mistakes. Let's review the five mistakes."

The players chanted in unison, "Fumbles . . . busted plays . . . intercepted passes . . . blocked punts . . . offsides."

Gaither added, "They've got a passing team, so let's rush that passer and intercept. This is open season on Wildcats!"

Another ear-splitting, "Hubba, Hubba!"

Gaither's lips drooped and tears streamed from his eyes as he mentioned a player who had died earlier in the season from injuries he had suffered in practice. His voice barely audible, Gaither said, "I don't like to mention this, boys, because it just tears me to pieces . . . Oliver Joyce was a Rattler."

Silence filled the room.

"Joyce gave everything for the Rattler squad. He lived and died like a Rattler." Gaither swallowed and dried his eyes. Then, speaking like the son of a Methodist minister that he is, he surmised, "He's upstairs now. We've made him happy for nine games. Let's make him happy tonight. I'm asking you to do this for me."

Still another "Hubba, Hubba!"

"Now let's pray to the Man Upstairs," Gaither said softly. Officials were pounding at the door signifying game time, but Gaither ignored them.

"O Good Lord, will You watch upon us and take care of us tonight? You have taken one of us early this season for what reason we do not know," Gaither said, his voice breaking. "But he is with You now and we know that we have made him happy up to now. We would like to make him happy tonight. Help us to do this, O Lord, who has given us sunshine and health, happiness and smiles. Give us strength tonight. Amen."

The squad barked its traditional, "We have wounded them. We have wounded them. They have fallen beneath our feet. They shall not rise. Allah!" The team charged out of the dressing room and defeated their opponent 28–7. The victory gave Jake Gaither his 120th victory against 20 losses over fifteen years and, presumably, Oliver Joyce happiness.

2

An Eye for Old KC

There will always be disadvantaged people;
not black, not white, just people. . . .
and Knoxville College must be the catalyst
to prepare them to meet their own destiny.

—ROBERT L. OWENS, III
former president
Knoxville College

Alonzo Smith Gaither, a sixteen-year-old boy from Middlesboro, Kentucky, arrived at Knoxville College in Knoxville, Tennessee, in the fall of 1919 to finish four years of high school. Knoxville College, which was founded in 1875 by Northern missionaries, operated an elementary school and high school in conjunction with its program in higher education.

In many ways, Knoxville College offered stability to young Gaither who, as a child, had lived in more than a dozen rural communities in Tennessee and Kentucky. Jake was born April 11, 1903, in Dayton, Tennessee. His father, Rev. A. D. Gaither, was a Methodist minister and as such was frequently assigned to a different church, mostly in small mining communities. By the time Mrs. Gaither and the five children established roots, it was time to move again. When Jake was sent off to school, the family was living in Middlesboro, Kentucky. Knoxville College, at least for Jake, put an end to the nomadic lifestyle; it also offered him a pristine environment, a nickname, the opportunity to meet his future wife, and fond memories.

"The longer I live, the more thankful I am that I went to that little school," he says now, almost fifty years after graduation. "I learned a sense of decency, of gratitude, of fineness, and of ethics. Knoxville College gave you a sense of values that I don't believe many schools give people. You learned the right things to say, you learned modesty, you learned appreciation of worth, and you learned to recognize merit in other people. You learned to evaluate people—to get a sense of values that has been practiced. I run into so many people who have no deep sense of morals—people who got a price tag on them, who'd sell their soul. I want to find the man who has no price tag on him. I'm not for sale. In high school I used to tell my boys that there are certain things a Knoxville College man won't do. You know, to this day I expect better conduct out of Knoxville College men than I do anybody else."

Today, Knoxville College has an enrollment of approximately one thousand students, about seven hundred more than when Gaither attended. It sits on thirty-nine acres of rolling hills, only a few miles from the University of Tennessee. Some of the dormitories are coeducational and upperclass women have unrestricted hours.

In Jake's day, the school was unusually strict, even when compared with other schools of that period. Knoxville was operated by the United Presbyterian Church, U.S.A., and many of its regulations reflected the wishes of the missionaries in power. Among the rules were the following:

No student will be allowed to remain in the school whose character may be such as will corrupt others.

The use of tobacco in any form is prohibited. Swearing and all improper language are also prohibited.

Students leaving grounds without the consent of the faculty render themselves liable to discipline.

Every student is expected to have his own Bible and dictionary.

No newspapers will be read on the Sabbath.

Students should avoid arriving on the Sabbath, and no baggage will be allowed to leave the grounds on that day.

Knoxville College is a private institution and therefore claims the privilege of eliminating from the institution at any time any student considered unsatisfactory without necessarily giving an explanation for dismissal.

Knoxville College occupied twenty-five acres during the 1920s, excluding the sixty-acre farm that adjoined the campus. Without exception, students spent part of their day working, either on the farm or campus. Gaither received his nickname as a result of an arrangement he and his dorm mates had to keep their residence hall clean. Each student would alternate cleaning the room and hallway; those who happened to be off that day would order the working student around. They would snap, "Jake, do this," or "Jake, do that," substituting "Jake" for the student's name. Gaither was the youngest of this coterie and, after the others graduated, the name stuck with him.

When his younger brother, Alexander, enrolled later, he became known around campus as Little Jake. Gaither says, "I like the name Jake better than I like the name Alonzo." And with a smile he adds, *"Alonzo* sounds like the name of a piano player."

Another name acquired by Gaither because of his fierce debating style and his role as the leader of several campus protests was "the Stormy Petrel." In four years Gaither lost only one debate, which he attributes to a weak partner. From 1923 to 1926 alone, Knoxville won seven of its eight debates. Gaither was unusually eloquent, prompting his audience to second his points with shouts of, "That's right!" To this day he has a rich baritone voice and a deliberate manner of speaking.

"I remember his first debate," says Sadie Robinson Gaither, a Knoxville College graduate whom Gaither married in 1931. "He and Tom Love were debating away. They [other students] said there was no chance for us to win the one on the road, with that freshman on the team. But about midnight the campus bell started ringing, signifying news of victory in that road debate. And it was like a football celebration—a parade the next day and everything." Jake had taken the affirmative in "The Philippines should be granted absolute independence."

Mrs. Gaither says, "I never thought he would be a football coach. He was always running his mouth, and I thought maybe he'd be a lawyer."

Jake was as sagacious and charming off-stage as on, in the opinion of his future wife, and the scuttlebutt was that Gaither had more than his share of women.

"He was no angel, yet he wasn't a reprobate either,"

Sadie says. "I would guess that Jake had plenty of girls on the side, but I would guess, too, that I was always number one."

The 1926 school yearbook had this to say about Gaither: "He is aspiring for the ministry, a good candidate, a deep and quick thinker. Sadie Mae can tell you how he stands with the ladies." There was at least one period in which Sadie had her doubts. She had taken a brief trip home and on her return she was greeted with a rumor—at least that is what Jake called it—that her boyfriend had been sending love letters to another girl on campus. Jake, eager to prove his innocence, demonstrated the various ways he could write and suggested that anyone could have forged his name. "He could explain his way out of anything," Sadie says now.

Gaither had numerous opportunities to explain his way out of situations, some of which threatened to get him dismissed from school.

Willis Weatherly, a former teammate and now manager of a housing development in Cincinnati, Ohio, remembers one short-lived rebellion.

"On Sundays we'd have Y.P.C.U. [Young People's Christian Union] service," Weatherly recalls. "On one occasion Jake and I decided to rake the administration on some of its rules. Dean Telford immediately accused us of 'throwing mud from behind the throne,' meaning that we were using the service to express our grievances. We were summoned before a faculty group and we apologized for our method, but still reiterated our belief that the college had been unfair."

To fully appreciate the import of the "mud from behind

the throne" remark, it is necessary to picture Dean Herbert M. Telford, who received his Ph.D. from Princeton. He wore three-piece suits and was as bald as he was pompous. The wire-rim glasses that perched on the tip of his nose left the impression that he was not just looking down at his glasses, he was also looking down at you. Every spring Telford would tell a student assembly: "Of late I have noticed that quite a few of the students are congregating in front of the main building and along the lower walk before McMillan Chapel. I wish you would not do this."

One such lecture was rudely interrupted one day. A student rocked to one side, tilted his gluteus maximus, and released a loud crackling sound. Undaunted, the magniloquent Telford looked the young man in the eye and said, "It is better to suppress a poot than to appear irreverent."

The students were unable, or unwilling, to suppress their laughter.

Nor did Gaither suppress his zeal for protesting.

About three hundred students decided to boycott classes one year until they were permitted to hold dances on campus. School officials believed dancing was tantamount to heresy. A poll of black ministers made public in 1926 disclosed that although 60 percent of the clergymen surveyed approved of football, baseball, fishing, and tennis, only 4 percent favored dancing. Opinion polls notwithstanding, the students persisted. A few days later, the president of the college wired the students' parents asking that they compel their children to sign an agreement to end the boycott or withdraw from school. Sadie's

brother, who was paying her tuition, wired her the following message: "Sign or you walk home. Chase City, Virginia, is a long way from Knoxville."

The boycott was broken in a matter of days.

On another occasion, Gaither sprang to the defense of
a recently dismissed black instructor whom he thought
had been summarily fired. The experience proved to be
didatic.

"One of the black teachers taught biology," he recalls.
"We all loved him. Then one year he didn't return. We
protested by writing letters and generally getting the
message across to the administration. Finally the president called a few of us in. We knew he had been trying
to get the college accredited. To do this he had to submit
the qualifications of the teachers.

"This biology teacher had represented himself as having a master's degree from Ohio State. In trying to establish his credentials, the president had obtained a letter
from Ohio State saying he had no master's degree. We
tucked our tails and crawled out of there. It taught me a
great lesson—never jump too fast at conclusions. The
president was trying to protect the man by not telling us
why he was not coming back."

In addition to being a leader of campus rebellions and
an accomplished debater, Gaither was active in many
other activities. He was president of the Sabbath Class,
editor of the yearbook, a member of the newspaper staff,
a choir member, vice president of the YMCA, president
of the college forum, and president of the senior class.
Gaither's father first objected to his playing football, but
eventually acquiesced. Rev. Gaither saw his son play once

and his acquiescence quickly transformed into euphoria. Jake was playing defense when an opponent broke away for what appeared to be an easy touchdown. Jake quickly caught up with him and stopped him with a diving tackle. Rev. Gaither stood up and yelled, "That's my boy. That's my boy."

Knoxville College permitted high school students to play on the college team in their junior and senior years. Jake played a total of six years on teams that accumulated a record of 16 wins, 12 defeats, and 1 tie. He played baseball two years, but the school did not have a basketball team or gymnasium. Ironically, the man who was later to become famous for having coached black players, never played for a black coach himself; all but three of his teachers were white.

Claude "Shorty" Cowan, later a successful physician in Washington, D.C., and a member of Knoxville's board of trustees, was quarterback during most of Gaither's years at Knoxville. He says, "Jake has always been an emotional guy. He always shook up guys. Although I was captain of the team, we all looked to Jake for guidance. We looked to him for his judgment more than his playing ability."

Willis C. Weatherly, another teammate, recalls, "He was a tough, forceful competitor. Just as he coached to win, he played to win. Crying was not unlike him; after we'd lose, he would often cry. I played four years with him and I played right tackle. I believe—I'm not sure—he played on the left side. He had a trick knee and it would jump out on him. He'd put it back in and keep on playing."

There was not enough football equipment to go around.

"If a player got hurt and came off the field, he had to give his shoulder pads to someone else," says Leo B. Marsh, a guard who later became assistant executive director of the National Board of YMCAs. "You bought your own shoes and on game day the guys would sit around looking mad and ugly. We called it our game face."

Game face and all, Jake was a starter at left end. He was All-Conference, but was less than spectacular on offense, catching only one touchdown pass in his career. Knoxville's favorite plays were the end-around and the old Statue of Liberty play. Players played both offense and defense in those days and, unlike today, the rules gave a decided advantage to the defensive team. For example, once a pass receiver was 20 yards past the line of scrimmage, pass interference did not apply. By the time Jake was a senior, a 5-yard penalty was assessed if more than one pass fell incomplete on the same series of downs.

The Aurora, the school newspaper, said Gaither "is faster than ever and his defensive work is still noticeable. He is also good on the receiving end of the pass."

There were no huddles then and signals were called at the line of scrimmage. Knoxville developed a system whereby a person on the sideline would record every number an opposing quarterback would call and attempt to correlate it with the play being run. It got so that the defensive team could anticipate some plays successfully. But there were some teams that could have given Knoxville their playbook and it wouldn't have helped. One such team was Tuskegee Institute of Alabama—"The Tuskegee Machine." From 1923 to 1928, Tuskegee was unbeaten in 45 games, having won 41 of them. From 1928 to 1931, they won 28 and lost 3. The 45-game mark is still the second longest unbeaten streak in history; Morgan State (now the University of Maryland–Eastern Shore) holds the record by virtue of having played 54 games from 1931 to 1938 without a defeat.

Knoxville players joked among themselves that they would end Tuskegee's dominance in the Southern Intercollegiate Athletic Conference. But the team got a better laugh when Alexander, Jake's younger brother, played behind him at end. Jake injured his ankle in one game and was rolling over in pain as teammates gathered around him. Alexander, meantime, simply ignored his brother's discomfort and inserted himself into the lineup without even consulting the coach.

Even as a student Jake loved football. In an article written for the school newspaper in his sophomore year, titled "Benefits Derived from Football," he said:

"Because of my love for football it might be impossible for me to be a fair and impartial critic of the game. But I feel justified in giving some of the benefits to be derived from the game, as I myself both feel and see them.

"A certain writer once said that the sin of the soul is selfishness and hate, and the sin of the mind is ignorance and untruth. I feel safe in saying that the sin of the body is weakness and disease, which saps the very vitality of manhood. Football, in the first place, develops the body. I know of no other game in which physical improvement is more evident than it is in football. The finest specimens of physical manhood in the world are to be found on the gridiron.

"However, physical development is not the only good

to be derived from the game. There is a moral value in the game that is far more vital and far reaching in its effect. A football player learns the value of cooperation. Unity is an essential factor in the game. There must be a team of eleven men, working together for the accomplishment of one specific end. A player must sacrifice personal gain and glory to become of this unit which represents the ideals of his school. He must likewise play the game fair and square, which develops a respect for the other fellow's rights. This is called sportsmanship. One of the greatest and most honorable compliments that can be paid to a player is, 'He is a good sport'—one who can stand the gaff, take the punishment, bump the bumps, and emerge from the conflict, conqueror or conquered, with the realization that he has played the game fair and square and has done his level best.

"Friendship formed with players under these conditions is dear and is the kind that lasts, because it is made under severe strain, in the heart of battle, and when a man's blood is up. The pal-like confidence and good fellowship that I have enjoyed with the fellows on the gridiron amply compensate for any hardships, bumps, and knocks that I might have received there."

An average student academically, Gaither graduated from Knoxville College in June 1927 with a major in social science and a minor in language. Forty-eight years later he was invited back to deliver the Founder's Day speech.

"I came to Knoxville College from the foothills of the Cumberland Mountains," he said. "I brought little with me except the background of a good home and the love of good parents who wanted me to get a good, solid education. It was here that I made my lifelong friends, treasured through the years. It was here that I met my mate. In brief, I owe so much to Knoxville College."

The speech was not one of Jake's more rousing performances. A better one, in the view of Lee Render, a former schoolmate and now an attorney in Cincinnati, Ohio, was made when as a student Gaither went before the student body before Homecoming, walked to the edge of the stage, winked, and said, "Give an eye for ol' KC." The students loved it.

Shortly before he graduated from Knoxville College, Jake Gaither's dream of becoming a minister was ended by an act of God. During his senior year, Rev. Gaither died and Jake's help was needed to keep the family viable. So, in 1927, just out of Knoxville, Gaither accepted a job as instructor at Henderson Institute, a high school operated by the Methodist church in Henderson, North Carolina. He taught math, civics, and debating and was coach of the football team.

"The first year we didn't win a game," Jake says. "We played eight games, we lost eight games. I was smart, you know, I knew everything. I don't think we scored a touchdown. Then the second year, we tied five games and lost three. I could generate a defense, but I couldn't get an offense going to save my neck. The third year we started winning. We ran everybody out of North Carolina. [Over the next six years, Gaither's teams lost only six games.]

"I had never seen a basketball game before. They didn't play basketball at my school when I finished and they didn't have a gymnasium. I saw my first basketball game in a tobacco warehouse in North Carolina. I didn't have basketball the first year I went to Henderson. I didn't know a thing about basketball, so I said, 'We don't need basketball.' The demand for basketball was so great then, the boys wanted to start a team. So I had a friend at another school who did know the game. He told me about basketball, I studied the rule book, and we put up a basketball goal outdoors. In three years we had a championship basketball team. We begged enough money to build a gymnasium at the high school. I had more success as a basketball coach than as a football coach.

"We got things to jell at the little high school. We won championships in football, basketball, and track. That's how I got into coaching. I even coached girls' basketball. Yeah, I got all the pretty girls in school out there. I got so I loved coaching. So much so that I figured nothing could stop me and that I was an iron man who could work all day and all night. I drove the bus, officiated basketball, and coached."

Jake's rivals were less than happy over his success.

An amendment to prohibit the state's two dozen private schools from being eligible for the state championship was introduced at a meeting of conference coaches in 1934. When the vote was taken, the measure was one vote shy of the two-thirds required by the association's bylaws. Yet the conference Commissioner ruled that the vote had carried, thus private schools, including Henderson Institute, would be disqualified from further competition. Gaither, after being recognized, was allowed to count the ballots himself. Then he read the section of the bylaws governing such changes, noting that a two-thirds majority was required; he pointed out that the motion to amend the bylaws was one vote short of the necessary margin. The commissioner of the conference wanted to put the matter to another vote immediately, but Gaither, clutching an old copy of the bylaws, pointed out that the issue could not be voted on again at the same meeting.

Jake recounted the details of the Winston-Salem meeting to E. B. Ray, a sportswriter for the *Norfolk Journal and Guide,* a black weekly. The executive committee of the association subsequently voted to suspend Gaither from coaching during the 1934–35 basketball season because he had disclosed the ouster effort to the press. With Gaither on the bench, his team still won the state championship, prompting sportswriters to dub his team "the Coachless Wonders."

The next season the "wonders" were indeed coachless, because Jake left Henderson for St. Paul Polytechnical Institute in Lawrenceville, Virginia.

Gaither was unsuccessful at St. Paul, but while there he made an important contact that eventually led to his joining the staff of Florida A&M. He had been studying each summer at Ohio State University toward his master's degree in physical education and health. By then he had married Sadie, his college sweetheart, and they spent each summer in a rooming house near the campus in Columbus. They met another roomer, William M. Bell, the former Ohio State tackle and then head football coach at Florida A&M. Gaither obtained his M.S. degree in the summer of 1937, and Bell invited him to join the staff as backfield coach and head basketball coach that fall. From 1937 through 1941, Florida A&M won 34 games, lost 5, and tied 5. Then in 1942, while still an assistant coach, Gaither was hospitalized, and for a while everyone gave him up for dead.

3

Rendezvous with Death

On a warm spring day in 1942, a decision had to be made quickly at Vanderbilt Hospital in Nashville, Tennessee. Jake Gaither, who had been driven up by ambulance from Tallahassee, was unconscious, only hours away from death. Dr. Earl T. Odom, a former schoolmate of Gaither's at Knoxville College and then a member of the faculty at Meharry Medical College, along with Dr. Cobb Pilcher, a well-known surgeon in Nashville, huddled in the hallway with Sadie Gaither.

Each moment grew increasingly crucial.

The physicians told Mrs. Gaither that they believed her husband had a brain tumor, although X-rays did not show it. Some other method had to be employed to detect the tumor and only then could it be removed. They said she had two options and she didn't have long to make up her mind. Even after she had made her choice, they told her, there would still be no guarantee that Gaither would live. One choice, they said, was carefully to make an incision around Jake's skull, lift the top, and try to find the tumor. The other alternative, then a relatively new technique, was to crack Gaither's skull and pump air into his head, which would force the tumor to the back of his head, thus making it easier to X-ray.

Sadie chose the latter. Within moments Jake Gaither was wheeled into the operating room. Beneath the bright lights and costly medical instruments, he underwent the operation. Lodged at the base of the skull, near the top of the spinal cord, were two malignant brain tumors. Jake Gaither had cancer of the brain.

Gaither had been complaining of headaches since March, after he coached Florida A&M to its first conference basketball championship. After returning from the tournament in Tuskegee, Alabama, several physicians had diagnosed his condition as Ménière's syndrome, a disorder characterized by swelling, vomiting, progressive deafness attributed to an effusion of blood into the inner ear (semicircular canal), and nausea. Usually the disorder disrupts one's sense of equilibrium.

"One thing you don't have to worry about," one specialist told Gaither. "You don't have to worry about a brain tumor."

The fact that Gaither had any illness was discovered accidentally. About a month after the basketball tournament in Tuskegee, Gaither, who had been selected to become dean of men the following year in addition to his football duties, was returning from a meeting at Hampton Institute in Hampton, Virginia, with the current dean of men.

"Coming back I got double vision," Jake says. "Instead of seeing one car, I saw two. Instead of seeing one white line, I saw two. Since I had to do all the driving [the dean of men was a nondriver], I tied a handkerchief around my head so that I could see out of one eye. Then I saw one line and one car. I struggled back to Florida, and they put me in the hospital and kept treating me for Ménière disease. I was losing weight constantly. I was really dying and they were feeding me through my veins. I went down to one hundred thirty-five from one hundred seventy-five. That's when my wife called Earl Odom.

"He was a doctor of internal medicine and uncanny on diagnosis. I was semiconscious. He comes here—he was teaching at Meharry in Nashville—talked to my wife at the breakfast table and practically diagnosed my case before he came to the hospital. He came to the hospital, took a little instrument and looked into my eyes—he never touched me—took Sadie out in the hallway and said, 'Jake's got a brain tumor and the only thing that can save him will be an operation.' He arranged for me to be taken to Vanderbilt. Odom had a friend who was a brain surgeon at Vanderbilt University named Cobb Pilcher. They tell me that Odom had a conference with the doctor and said, 'Doctor, what is this operation gonna cost? She doesn't have much money. She has spent so much already.' Pilcher said, 'Well, I usually get a thousand dollars for this kind of operation.' Odom said, 'She can afford to pay a hundred dollars.' The doctor said, 'Alright. When I'm operating on a rich man, I charge him a rich man's fee. When I'm operating on a poor man, I charge him a poor man's fee. And I try to give them both the same service.'"

Gaither spent six weeks recovering from the operation, most of that time at a Seventh-Day Adventist hospital across town. Each day brought excruciating pain. His legs were massaged during the day and his nights were spent tossing from side to side to avoid sleeping on the back of his head, part of which had been removed by surgery.

By the time Gaither, his wife still at his side, was ready to be discharged, his hospital bill was $1,400. There was some question as to whether Jake, who had planned to visit his brother in Columbus, Ohio, had enough money to travel north. The problem was solved only because he had received about $400 from students and faculty at Florida A&M. There was still another problem: How could Jake, still weak from surgery, travel to Ohio? His meager funds could only provide transportation via bus or train. The former would have caused undue strain for so sick a man; the latter would have been equally painful because blacks were not allowed to ride in Pullman cars under the Jim Crow laws then in effect. Dr. Pilcher, a white millionaire, arranged for Gaither to be accommodated in a Pullman car by telephoning railroad officials and saying he had "a patient" who desperately needed a place in a coach.

Meanwhile, Pilcher forwarded Jake's medical records to a contact in Columbus, where Jake would be living for a while. The physician told Gaither upon arrival that the fee for treatment was $16 a visit, but that he would treat him free if Jake agreed to appear at a clinic operated by Ohio State University's medical school.

"He took me in front of his class one day," Gaither later related. "He says, 'Now, there's something unusual about this. What is it?' They gave one thing after another. He said, 'No, that's not it.' He said, 'In all my practice of medicine, I have never seen this type of tumor in a Negro. It's unusual that a Negro has this type of tumor.' I told

Odom about it later, and he said, 'That's a lie. The trouble is blacks have died with this type of tumor and never got the proper diagnosis.' "

The decision to send Gaither to Columbus rather than back to Tallahassee was made in an effort to keep him away from the temptation of going back to coaching too soon. After a few months with Alexander (Little Jake), who later became director of the Civil Rights Division of the Highway Department in the United States Department of Transportation, Jake persuaded his brother to take him to see a football game. Little Jake wrapped his brother in a blanket, placed him in a wheelchair and took him to see a game between the Michigan and Ohio State freshmen teams. Jake seemed revitalized by the game, and his younger brother and everyone else knew from his expression that it wouldn't be long before Gaither would be back in Tallahassee and, naturally, on the sidelines.

By January, Jake Gaither had returned home via train. He was stronger than before, but still weak and suffering from the aftereffects of his operation. He had occasional spells of blindness, but his vision and strength slowly returned. While Jake was in Columbus, Sadie had taken in USO boarders, sold their old car, and performed part-time work to keep the family solvent. Now she returned to her job as an English instructor and Jake returned to work on a part-time basis, teaching economics and sociology. He still walked with the aid of a cane and his body was not totally coordinated. Leon Watts, a student, lived in with the Gaithers and helped with the household chores.

"When I went back on the payroll, we were in better

financial shape than before I went in the hospital," Gaither says. "How in God's name she [Sadie] did it, I don't know; she only earned sixty-seven dollars a month as a substitute teacher. From then on I told her to handle the finances."

And Jake was able to handle himself.

4

Breaking Ground

Jake Gaither missed the 1942 and 1943 seasons and served as an "advisory coach" to Herman N. "Buck" Neilson during the 1944 season. He was studying alcoholism at Yale during the summer of 1945 when he received a telegram from William H. Gray, president of Florida A&M: "Dear Jake," it read. "Since it is now August and we can't get anybody else to coach the football team, it looks like you will have to take over." Jake did take over and 1945 proved a historic year for the school, as well as marking the end of World War II and the death of Adolf Hitler, Benito Mussolini, and President Franklin Roosevelt.

In Tallahassee, Jake Gaither, having been named head football coach and athletic director, was about to begin a distinguished career. Gaither solidified a winning tradition that had begun under his predecessor, William M. Bell, the former All–Big Ten tackle at Ohio State.*

---

*Bell was one of a number of blacks who played football at Northern universities in the early 1900s and afterwards coached at predominantly black colleges in the South. Bell was first-string tackle at Ohio State, becoming the first black to play for the school since the late 1800s. He was later president of the Central Intercollegiate Athletic Conference, head coach and athletic director at North Carolina A&T (1946–57), and is presently a member of the NCAA's executive committee and assistant to the chancellor at Fayetteville (N.C.) State College.

Records have been kept at Florida A&M since 1933. That year the team won 4 and lost 1. The next two years, FAMU was outscored by its opponents, while accumulating 4–2–0 and 4–4–1 records respectively. Bell arrived in 1936 and had the following record:

Year	Won	Lost	Tied
1936	2	4	1
1937	6	1	1
1938	8	0	0
1939	6	2	1
1940	6	1	3
1941	8	1	0
1942	9	0	0
	45	9	6

"Jake was a very good backfield coach," says Bell, the only college coach under whom Gaither has worked. "He was a good strategist, although he had difficulty at St. Paul. St. Paul didn't put any money into football. He [Jake] hadn't won but one game in sixteen. I had worked as an assistant at Howard [University] and I knew St. Paul wasn't putting any money into it. But Jake had an excellent high school record in North Carolina. He taught a good game of football. His philosophy seemed to be sound and that's why I invited him to join me."

Bell laughs as he reflects on those days. "Back then," he says chuckling, "they would ask a man teaching mathematics or history, 'How about coaching the football team?' He didn't have playing or coaching experience and just went out and coached the team the best he could."

Under Bell's leadership, Florida A&M won its first conference and national championships. His 1938 team scored 189 points and was not scored on until the last game of the season, when FAMU defeated Kentucky State University in the Orange Blossom Classic, 9–7. His teams also won the conference and national championships in 1937 and 1942. Bell, now a retired lieutenant colonel in the Air Force Reserve, left FAMU to join the armed forces during World War II.

"In the spring of 1943 I took all my boys and marched them from college to Mayberry Field, now the airport today," Bell recalls. "I signed them all up, and when they were called, I went with them."

Buck Neilson, the lone coach in 1944, left FAMU to join the staff at Hampton Institute in Virginia thus making way for Jake.

Jake Gaither began work in a climate of racial hostility, a period in which blacks were treated as less than human, and every tool—legal and extralegal—was utilized to deny blacks their constitutional rights as citizens. Southern whites boasted, "We don't hate niggers—we think everyone ought to have one." Ministers told their congregations that God didn't intend the races to mix; otherwise He would have made everyone the same color. Blacks were kept segregated in public facilities; there were "white" and "colored" water fountains in most department stores, and the public schools were separate and unequal. Oklahoma had segregated telephone books, Mississippi had segregated Coca-Cola machines, black witnesses in Atlanta's courts were not allowed to swear on the same Bible as whites, and Florida school officials even segregated the textbooks when they were kept in storage.

Tallahassee was probably more racist than many major cities in the South.

Mrs. Rosa Parks, a black seamstress in Montgomery, Alabama, touched off a series of protests in the South, including Tallahassee, on December 1, 1955, when she refused to give up her seat to a white man on a crowded bus. She was arrested and a then-obscure twenty-seven-year-old minister by the name of Martin Luther King, Jr., mobilized the black community in protest of this unconstitutional action. A year later the United States Supreme Court ordered the Montgomery buses desegregated.

Elsewhere throughout the Deep South, blacks also began defying Jim Crow ordinances and state laws. Rev. C. K. Steele, president of the Tallahassee chapter of the NAACP, spearheaded a bus boycott after two women students at Florida A&M were arrested May 28, 1956, for sitting next to a white woman on a crowded bus.

The Tallahassee city council moved to circumvent the Supreme Court decision by enacting a city ordinance that required bus drivers to seat riders in numbered seats on the basis of weight distribution, health factors, and other considerations. Actually the new law was a subterfuge to keep the city's segregation laws intact. Rev. Steele and a committee called the Negro Inter-Civil Council against Cities Transit Company led a boycott that was about 75 percent effective. The chamber of commerce countered with a "Ride the Bus" campaign among whites. In the end, however, the bus company had to suspend service because its predominantly black ridership stayed off the buses.

The black groups organized a car pool to transport residents who needed transportation (about a third of Tallahassee's forty thousand residents were black). On October 21, 1956, the boycott leaders were found guilty of operating an illegal public transportation system without a city permit or "for hire" license. Summoning what he called "divine guidance," Circuit Judge John Rudd fined twenty-one blacks $55 each and gave them a sixty-day jail sentence—the maximum under law. He then suspended the sentence saying, "I hope each of you will be Christian enough to abide by the law."

When the bus firm resumed operations, city policemen began arresting bus drivers who failed to enforce the city ordinance that, in effect, maintained segregated seating. U.S. District Judge Dozier Devane, at a hearing held late one night in his home, issued a temporary order instructing the city to stop arresting drivers and prohibited it from interfering with bus operations or revoking the firm's license.

The focus then shifted from the courts to violence. A shotgun blast damaged a black grocery, and rocks were thrown into the homes of four black leaders, including that of Rev. Steele. Some days later, a four-foot cross, wrapped in Spanish moss and soaked in kerosene, was burned in front of Rev. Steele's church; his house was later bombed. The city continued to fine black students from Florida A&M and white students from cross-town Florida State University as well as city residents for challenging the segregation laws. Eventually, the city complied with the court rulings.

The list of indignities inflicted upon blacks in Tallahassee and the rest of the country is long. And it was in this atmosphere that Jake Gaither lived. Gaither did not actively involve himself in social causes—unless you classify his work as a coach and leader at Florida A&M as such. Instead he concentrated on uplifting a small, largely ignored black college to the level where it is now, known throughout the world, largely as a result of his and his pupils' accomplishments.

"When I came here in 1937, we had a squad of thirty-eight men—fourteen of those boys were from Ohio alone," Gaither remembers. "There weren't over a half-dozen Florida boys on the squad. That was the condition in Florida. Most coaches in the black high schools were vocational men; they weren't hired as coaches or on their ability as football players, but because they were usually high-paid teachers and had more time. So, whether they could coach or not, they were the coaches. The result was that the boys in Florida were poorly developed in fundamentals.

"Well, Florida A&M got the best athletes wherever they were. In 1937, we lost one game. The next year we won the conference and national championships. That was the year we hit the jackpot [8–0–0]. Still, the majority of our boys were from out of state. We had three or four outstanding boys from Florida. We had to go out of the state to recruit; we went to seven states and the District of Columbia. All during this time I wanted to see the Florida boys have a chance to play. I felt that since this was a state-supported school, the boys in the state ought to have a chance.

"In 1946 I realized the only way we could upgrade the coaching in the state was to train them in fundamentals.

Also, the state of Florida passed a law that nobody could coach in the state unless he had so many hours in health and physical education. And that threw out all the vocational teachers, and our boys began to move into coaching positions."

When openings occurred, Gaither was usually consulted for a recommendation, and invariably he would suggest one of his former players. This pattern continued until about 95 percent of the head coaches in black high schools were Florida A&M graduates. Gaither persuaded each coach to install Florida A&M's play-calling system. Consequently, when the players went from high school to Florida A&M, they already knew the plays and Gaither could direct his attention elsewhere.

From the outset, all of Gaither's assistants have been Florida A&M graduates, a fact not lost on the high school coaches. Each high school coach would funnel his best players to his old coach to help his Alma Mater while simultaneously improving the prospect of Gaither remembering him when he needed another assistant at FAMU.

FAMU had so much talent in those days that if a back couldn't reach the line of scrimmage in eight-tenths of a second, he would be converted into a lineman. There was no room on the roster for all the state's outstanding athletes, let alone the average ones. It made about as much sense for a person of average ability to try out for the squad as it would to enter a child's plastic horse in the Kentucky Derby. One year, for example, Gaither had starting backs who could run the 100-yard dash in 9.1, 9.3, and 9.4 seconds respectively. "You take a groundhog and

tie him up on Friday morning and don't give him anything to eat," Gaither says, smiling. "Then on Saturday
you untie him and pour kerosene on his tail—that's the
kind of speed I get from my boys."

When William Bell hired Gaither and Bell's brother,
Horace, who played with Bud Wilkerson at Minnesota, he
took them across the country to attend coaching clinics.
Gaither continued the habit with his assistants when he
took over. He didn't want black high school coaches to go
through the same thing, therefore in 1946 he opened his
own clinic, which was usually attended by more than one
hundred coaches from throughout the state. In the thirty
years of these clinics Jake had all the major coaches in to
direct sessions: Bear Bryant, Woody Hayes, Bobby Dodd,
Frank Broyles, Darrell Royal, Ara Parseghian, Frank
Howard, Ben Schwartzwalder, Frank Howard, Rip Engle,
Sid Gilman, and Bill Yeoman.

Gaither, in his first fifteen years, recruited heavily in the
North and East. He was on the road more than CBS's
Charles Kuralt. Then he started recruiting exclusively in
the state of Florida.

"In 1960 we stopped going out of the state of Florida,
and I'll tell you what caused it," he says. "I was in Pennsylvania recruiting, and we had been working hard all day.
I was at a boy's home waiting for the boy's father to come
home. I had the boy all ready to sign and come to Florida.
When we got ready to sign, the boy's father said, 'I don't
want him to go to Florida.' I said, 'What's the matter?' He
said, 'I don't want him to go South.' I said, 'We got a good
school down here, we have females on campus and he
wouldn't run into any trouble.' He said, 'You can't tell me

a thing about Florida, because I just left Alabama and I know the hell blacks catch in the South.'

"Well, I found myself trying to defend the South during the days of segregation and discrimination. I was fighting the Civil War all over. At that time, if we had a roster of sixty, you might find ten from Florida. Here I was in Pennsylvania trying to find a two hundred twenty-five-pound tackle when I could go out of my door and sneeze two or three two-hundred-twenty-five-pound tackles. So I thought about what Booker T. Washington said: 'Cast down your bucket where you are.' We have never traveled outside the state of Florida since. We have found these boys are just as good as other boys, and they play just as good a brand of football."

Gaither also carefully cultivated white coaches who worked for Southern white universities. When these white coaches came across an excellent black player, they would pass the word to Jake. And the players themselves applied; about 150 applicants a year would write Gaither to inquire about joining the squad, many of them from out of state. Each year the FAMU coaches would take two recruiting trips up and down the coasts of Florida. Any player who chose another school over Florida A&M would be reminded of that fact if his team played FAMU. "Whenever he gets that ball I want to see eleven men on him—hard but clean." Gaither would admonish. "Then I want all eleven men to say, 'Gee, I'm sorry you didn't come to Florida A&M.' "

Aside from physical retribution, players were also attracted to FAMU because it sponsored its own bowl game of sorts annually.

"Every time someone mentions Papa Jake Gaither, I think back to a newspaper cartoon of nearly twenty years ago," says Edwin Pope, sports editor of the *Miami Herald*. "It showed a football coach talking to a reporter. 'No, no,' the coach was saying thoughtfully. 'No bowl game for us this year. We've played our season. The boys need the extra time for their studies. They want to spend their holidays at home. And besides . . .' he paused as though looking for additional reasons, '. . . we haven't been invited!' " Said Pope, "They will never use Papa Jake in such a cartoon . . . A&M simply runs its own bowl for its own team."

Not exactly.

The Orange Blossom Classic is a regular-season game that draws about forty thousand spectators annually. FAMU, the host team, waits until late in the season to pick what it considers to be a top opponent. Although Gaither's twenty-five-year record consists of 203 wins, 36 losses, and 4 ties, his Orange Blossom Classic record is only 12 wins and 13 defeats—a fact that he says proves he didn't select patsies for opponents.

"I think that's the thing that made the Classic grow," he says. "The fact that the public believes that we will not pick a team for the Classic simply because we can beat them. We must have the most consistent football team in the country, because every year we have to play a top opponent. What team has had a record over thirty-six years that they could afford to play the last game of the season against the toughest team in the country and make the game interesting enough to draw forty thousand people? It stands to reason that we can't win most of the time.

As Dr. [former president George W.] Gore once said about the Classic, 'We want to have a team good enough to make the best team in the land play its best ball to beat us. And we have got to have it every year.'

"There are some teams that only have a good season every four years. We had never heard of Alcorn as a football team until a few years before I retired. Prairie View was a great team ten or eleven years ago; they have now gone into oblivion. Maybe they'll come out of it. But Florida A&M has had to have a team that could play the best team the last game of the season and not get run out of the ballpark."

The Orange Blossom Classic is the brainchild of J. R. E. Lee, Jr., who took over as the school business manager in 1924, the same year his father took over as president. The game was initiated in 1933, which was only eleven months after the Orange Bowl was inaugurated.

"I really conceived the idea because we used to play at Howard University in an annual Thanksgiving Day Classic," Lee says. "And I thought we could develop the same thing in Florida. We knew that a top-notch opponent would be the key to the success or failure, so our first opponent was Howard University of Washington, D.C. When we invited them they turned us down because they were playing Lincoln University [Pa.] on the Thursday night before our scheduled Classic, which was to be played two nights later.

"After being turned down by the Howard Athletic Association, I contacted Emmit J. Scott, secretary-treasurer at Howard and did a little bargaining. I told him I'd have a Pullman coach waiting in Atlantic City when they finished their Thursday game, and all they'd have to do would be to board it. They agreed. If they had turned down that offer, there would be no Classic today."

FAMU won that first game 9–6 in Myrtle Avenue Baseball Park in Jacksonville, Florida. The park, which seated two thousand, proved to be too small and the game was moved several years later to Tinker Field in Orlando, which had a seating capacity of six thousand. The game was later switched to the sixteen thousand–seat Phillips Field in Tampa, and in 1947 it was changed to the Orange Bowl in Miami. It is still held there, and twenty-two years after its inception, it is still successful.

5

Galloping Galimore

Black college football has been subjected to unwarranted and often scathing criticism over the years, primarily because black schools have not competed against white universities on a regular basis. Black coaches have retorted that their product has been and is as outstanding as that developed by any schools. Moreover, they point with pride to the numerous outstanding players they have sent to the professional ranks.

"We have to wait until our players reach pro ball," Gaither has said on many occasions, referring to the lack of competition between black and white colleges. "In pro ball I'll match my boys against anybody's."

The first Florida A&M player to excel in professional football was Willie Galimore, the fleet-footed running back for the Chicago Bears. But even Galimore's job was made easier by Paul "Tank" Younger of Grambling, the first player signed by the National Football League from an all-black college.

It was Willie Galimore who blazed the trail at Florida A&M for such stars as Bob Hayes, Hewritt Dixon, Carleton Oats, Roger Finnie, Al Denson, Ken Riley, Willie Lee, and Glen Edwards.

But when Galimore first arrived at FAMU, the only trail he blazed was one leading directly to the fourth team.

"He was fast, but he was long-gaited," Gaither says. "We had to shorten his stride so he could learn to start quicker. We also made him practice running in the sand with shorter steps."

Gaither also remembers teaching Galimore a lesson on punctuality.

"We used to have our scholarship boys do an hour's work every day," Jake recalls. "Galimore's job was to clean my office—sweep and dust it every morning. I came into the office one morning and it hadn't been swept or dusted, so I sent for Galimore. He told me that he was very sorry, but that he had overslept that morning. He promised me he wouldn't do it again. Two weeks later, the office was dirty again. I sent for Galimore. He said he had an assignment to get out in the library and that he just missed doing his job that morning. He promised me that it would never happen again.

"It did happen in another two weeks and I sent for Galimore. He looked through the door and said, 'Now, Coach . . .' I said, 'Stop right there; don't say another word. Now, if what you are going to say will make that broom hop out of the closet and go to sweeping this floor, and the dust rag get off that shelf and start cleaning this furniture, I want you to talk. Otherwise, don't say anything.' It was nine–fifteen. I said, 'At nine o'clock the president of the United States is in his office working. The president of this university is in his office working. And I'm in my office working. Why in the world can't you be working?'

"He went to work and we never had any more trouble

with Mr. Galimore cleaning up the office."

Nor did Gaither have any more trouble with him on the football field. Gaither says that Galimore, the only FAMU player to be selected All-America three times, was the best athlete he has ever coached.*

Galimore still holds seven school records that were established twenty years ago:

Longest touchdown run: 98 yards against Allen (Nov. 24, 1956)

Most touchdowns rushing in a season: 15 in 1956

Net yards rushing in a single game: 295 yards against Maryland State in 1954

Longest kickoff return: 87 yards against Bethune-Cookman (1956)

Most touchdowns in a season (tied with Al Frazier): 16 in 1956

Most touchdowns in one game: (4) against Tennessee State (1956)

Most points in one game: 24 against Tennessee State (1956)

As talented as Galimore was, he still did not possess the natural skill of his running mate, Al Frazier, who played in the Canadian Football League and, in 1961, 1962, and 1963, for the Denver Broncos. Both had speed—Galimore

---

*Ric Roberts of the *Pittsburgh Courier,* a black weekly, has over the years been responsible for polling black coaches to determine the All-America squad. AP, UPI, *Time, Playboy,* and the other major publications still ignore players at all-black colleges, as they have in the past, except in rare instances. Yet there can be no question that the record shows that these players are just as talented as players anywhere else in the country.

ran a 9.8 in the 100-yard dash and Frazier ran a 9.7—and either could score from any point on the field. Jake rates them as the best backfield combination he has ever coached. Frazier still holds the school season record for scoring—118 points—which was also tops in 1956 among black colleges. Both men scored 16 touchdowns each; Frazier also kicked point-after-touchdowns.

"Galimore was an extremely fine player and we were pretty close," says Frazier, who now lives in New York City. "I didn't have the build or weight to be the ballplayer he was. My style was a little different. I was better when I was past the defensive line and I was always a good receiver. Galimore was a good blocker and he was the kind of football player Jake had a hand in making. When I came to Florida A&M, I already had it."

The Chicago Bears drafted Galimore (as a future) in the fifth round of the 1956 draft, a year before he graduated. The story around Chicago, which was certainly apocryphal, was that Phil Handler, then a scout for the team's coaching staff, was on a fishing trip in Florida in the mid-1950s when a jockey told him that FAMU had the fastest, most elusive halfback in the country. Handler was said to have confirmed that Galimore had another year of eligibility and persuaded the Bears to draft Galimore—sight unseen.

The Bear's press brochure described Galimore as "something to watch." George Halas, the founder and coach of the team, says he sent Garland Grange—Red's brother—to Miami to watch FAMU play Maryland State in the 1954 Orange Blossom Classic. Florida A&M won 67–19. Galimore, a sophomore, gained 295 yards and scored 5 touchdowns, of which 2 were nullified.

"Galimore is an intelligent boy who has fine poise," Halas said after Willie joined the team in 1957. "He seldom makes the same mistake twice. He has grace and acceleration and can use the limp leg or the straight arm when necessary. We worked very hard with him to correct those fumbles, and he is fine, just fine. His college coach, Jake Gaither, told us he was pro material, and that's when we sent Grange down to Florida."

In his rookie year, Galimore—who was called Galloping Galimore, Wiggling Willie, and Willie the Wisp—became the fifth player in the team's history to score 4 touchdowns in one game (against the Los Angeles Rams). He finished the season with 538 yards, a 4.2 average; he scored 7 touchdowns, and was his team's second leading scorer, behind George Blanda.

His best season was 1961, when he picked up 707 yards on 153 carries, caught 33 passes for 502 yards, and returned 5 kickoffs for 82 yards. His best game was played September 22, 1962, when he rushed for 176 yards on 23 tries against the San Francisco 49ers.

Galimore, like Gale Sayers and O. J. Simpson, was an exciting player, the kind that could bring a crowd to its feet whenever he touched the ball. He was the kind of runner that Gaither says can cut on a dime and give you a nickle change. Unlike his off-field demeanor, Galimore was extroverted on the field, crashing footballs to the ground after he scored a touchdown. Jake says Galimore was the first to start that trend in the pros, and Gaither was livid when the antic was outlawed in 1969 among colleges.

"Willie Galimore was the first to bust the ball after scoring," Gaither said. "Willie carried the habit to pro football with the Chicago Bears. I've encouraged it all these years. When we score at A&M, I'm happy and the boys are happy. What does it hurt to fling the ball to the ground? We've been doing it for a decade and never ruined a football yet. So what if we did—I'd trade a football for a touchdown any day of the week." Asked why his players crashed the balls to the turf after scoring a touchdown, Gaither replied: "They're mad because there's no more running room left."

On July 26, 1964, Willie Galimore ran out of running room.

Galimore, twenty-nine years old, and a teammate, John Farrington, twenty-eight, died when Galimore's sun-roof Volkswagen sedan crashed about two and a half miles west of Rensselaer, Indiana, where the Bears were holding training camp. Farrington, an offensive end from Prairie View A&M College in Texas, had started in all the Bears' regular-season games the previous season, catching 21 passes for 335 yards and 2 touchdowns. Galimore was recovering from his third off-season knee operation and was "looking better than ever before since he's been with us," in the words of Assistant Coach Phil Handler.

The Bears were the defending NFL champions. Halas called the team together shortly after the tragedy and said, "I know we all share the same sad feelings. Something like this reaches the heart and makes everything else seem so petty. It is going to take a great deal of will-power to carry on, but I know you can do it. The greatest honor we can bestow on Willie and Bo is if you players would dedicate the season to them." The team voted in favor of honoring their former teammates, but the losses were not easily forgotten. At the next practice session an assistant coach was seen picking up a gum wrapper from the ground. When asked why, he replied: "Willie always had a habit of asking me if I had a stick of gum during practice and sometimes I would slip him one. Sunday when he asked, I dug into my pocket and pulled out half a stick. He took it and threw the wrapper on the ground. It was the same wrapper, and I just couldn't bear looking at it."

It was also a sad time for the players families. In addition to his wife, Galimore left three young children: Ronnie, aged seven; Fawndreta, age five; and Marlon, age four. Farrington's wife was expecting their first child. Galimore invariably called his wife in Chicago every night to take advantage of the lower telephone rates. But for some reason he called her at about one o'clock in the afternoon on the day he died.

The families' grief was compounded by erroneous press reports that indicated the two players were killed while trying to make it back for 11:00 P.M. curfew. The truth is that they were only a six- or seven-minute drive from their rooms at St. Joseph's College, and the accident happened around 10:30 P.M., a half-hour before curfew. Both players had been at the Rensselaer Country Club for dinner and had been watching a college track meet on television around 10:00 that night. Someone incorrectly told them that another segment of the track meet would be shown at 10:30, and the two tried to get to the dorms before the other part of the meet came on. Actually, no meet was scheduled, and had the two known this, they might have exercised more caution.

Police authorities estimated that Galimore's Volkswagen was traveling 55 miles per hour when the accident occurred. Jasper County Deputy Wayne Calloway said that had Galimore been familiar with the country road, he could have made the curve at an even higher speed. The VW struck the shoulder of the road, the rear wheels collapsed, and the two men were ejected through the top of the automobile, causing multiple skull fractures and internal injuries; the car rolled over them. Highway Patrol officials said an "S-curve" sign that had been posted near the spot where the accident occurred had been knocked down two weeks earlier in another accident and not been replaced.

Galimore left a legacy to football, nonetheless.

An all-league halfback in 1959, he won the Eisenhower Trophy as the most valuable player in the 1958 Armed Forces Game. In seven seasons he gained 2,985 yards rushing on 670 carries for 26 touchdowns, caught 87 passes for 1,201 yards and one touchdown—a 99-yarder in the 1958 season-opener.

More important, Galimore opened the door for other Florida A&M players.

6

The World's Fastest Human

After learning that several of his players had become envious of Bob Hayes, even to the point of calling him "Hollywood," Jake Gaither hastily called a team meeting for 7:30 P.M. in the school's gymnasium.

The players had been chatting jovially and engaging in guffaws before the coaches arrived. At 7:29 the rear doors opened quickly and Gaither walked in, his assistants in tow. Instantaneously the talking ceased. Gaither sauntered over to Hayes and excused him from the meeting. Just as Hayes was leaving through the door, Gaither was reaching his position in front of the room.

Gaither stared at the players, pausing long enough for everyone to undergo a quick self-examination.

"I hear some of you on this team might be a little jealous because of all the publicity Bob is getting," Gaither said with his deep resonant voice. "Don't you realize this is the fastest human in the world? Do you know that no human in history ever ran the one hundred-yard dash in 9.1? You boys ought to consider it an honor to play on the same team with him. I consider it an honor to coach him.

"But I'll tell you what. I'll tell you how you can get more publicity than this boy. I will tell you how to get your picture in the paper and on television. I'll tell you how you can make people forget they ever heard of Bob Hayes."

One player, unable to restrain himself any longer, asked "How coach?"

Deadpanned Gaither, "Outrun him."

That would have been some feat, for Hayes has been outrunning people since he was a student at Matthew Gibson High in Jacksonville, Florida. When he was a sophomore, Hayes told Bill Cannon, the track coach, that he could "outrun any of those clowns on the track team." And he did, defeating the team's top sprinter by 5 yards. Hayes enrolled at Florida A&M upon graduation and soon brought international recognition to the Tallahassee school—even more than Willie Galimore had produced through his exploits. He was unquestionably the fastest human in the world, having defeated the world's best sprinters and becoming the first human in the world to run the 100-yard dash in 9.1 seconds.* He won two gold medals in the 1964 Olympics and later became an outstanding wide receiver for the Dallas Cowboys before being traded to the San Francisco 49ers.

"If you locked twenty defensemen of the National Football League in a room with a police artist and asked them to reconstruct the features and appearance of the Dallas Cowboys' Bob Hayes, the resultant composite drawing would probably look more like Rutherford B. than Robert

---

*Hayes's 1963 record for the 100-yard dash was not bettered until eleven years later when Ivory Crockett of St. Louis ran it in nine seconds flat. However, Crockett's mark was tied in less than a year by Houston McTear, an eighteen-year-old high school student at Baker High School in Milligan, Florida. McTear is now generally considered the world's top sprinter because he has defeated most of the nation's other sprinters, including Crockett.

Hayes," wrote syndicated columnist Jim Murray. "There isn't one of these back-pedallers who could pick him out of a roomful of Malaysians the first try. They get the same look at him as a hit-and-run victim of the driver on a dark night."

But Hayes's unorthodox style easily distinguishes him from other sprinters. He is knock-kneed and pigeon-toed; he wobbles when he runs, often spiking himself on the big toe.

"He's an ugly duckling sprinter who surprised us all," says Pete Griffin, Hayes's track coach at Florida A&M. "He's rewriting the book on sprinting styles." Hayes is about five feet eleven inches tall and weighs about 185 pounds. He has extremely thick muscles; only his ankles are small. Griffin says Hayes runs wide-legged because of his short, thick muscles and long legs. Consequently his feet land about twelve inches apart, about four inches wider than average.

John Underwood, writing in *Sports Illustrated,* said, "When Robert Lee Hayes runs you get the impression that cotter pins have come out and dowels loosened and that at the end of the race there will be sections of Bob Hayes—elbows, kneecaps, forearms—strewn out along the track like the Florida Keys."

Despite the brouhaha over Hayes's style, he is still the shortest distance between two points. Gordon Forbes, writing in *Sport* magazine, said, "Bob Hayes runs with his arms too high, toes too pigeoned, feet too wide—and speed too fast for any sprinter to beat."

Pete Griffin, Hayes's coach, did not attempt to alter Bob's style; he just tried to keep him in peak condition.

Hayes ran the way he wanted, yet every time he ran, he kept stumbling into obstacles that prevented him from officially being recognized as the world's fastest sprinter.

It should be remembered that Hayes went to FAMU on a football, not track, scholarship. But as a freshman he was overlooked on a team that won nine of its ten games, outscoring its opponents 515–73. The only freshman to start that year was Al Denson, an end who later starred for the Denver Broncos of the old American Football League. That same team defeated Benedict College, 60–0; Morris Brown, 64–0; Bethune-Cookman, 97–0; and South Carolina State, 80–0. So Hayes had to get his recognition elsewhere, which he did.

Bob ran a 9.3 in the 100-yard dash at a meet in Sioux Falls, South Dakota, equaling an NAIA record. Later that year, a race in the Trinidad Invitational was a preview of a string of misfortunes. Hayes, a sophomore, tied the world record for 200 meters (curve), but the time was not officially recognized because the event had not been previously listed in the meet's program. Then as a junior, Hayes ran a 9.1 at Coral Gables, Florida—his teammates Bob Paremore and Al Austin ran 9.2—but that accomplishment was nullified because the official starter used a .22-caliber pistol instead of the AAU- and NCAA-approved .32, from which smoke can be seen. Hayes finally ran an official 9.3 to share the world record with a dozen others, but before it could be accepted, Hayes's nemesis, Frank Budd, lowered the record to 9.2.

Hayes thought he had bettered Budd's new mark in the Florida A&M Relays when officials announced that he had been timed at an incredible 8.9. There was one problem:

When the track was remeasured, it was found to be six yards short. "At least we know we have the record for ninety-four yards," joked Gaither.

On June 21, 1963, Bob Hayes ran what finally became accepted as the world's record for the 100-yard dash. After bettering the world record of 9.2 on four occasions, Bob ran a blistering 9.1 at the AAU Championship in St. Louis on a sleek new rubberized track. But true to form, the record was not accepted until two days before Hayes was scheduled to compete in the 1964 Olympics.

Mrs. Mary Hayes, Bob's mother, and Jake Gaither were in Tokyo to see the speedster compete. They saw Hayes become the first person to run 110 meters in less than 10 seconds—he ran 9.9—but the record did not stand because of a considerable wind at Hayes's back; the wind was about twelve miles an hour, twice the allowable standard. Hayes did manage to tie the world record of 10 seconds flat in the finals, earning a gold medal in the process. One Japanese spectator was so impressed that he turned to an American and said, "I congratulate you," as though the entire United States were responsible. The congratulations, however misdirected, were premature. Hayes came from behind twice en route to leading his team to a gold medal in the 400-meter relay race. As anchor man, he received the baton in sixth place, made up 10 yards, and won impressively.

The Olympics crowned a brilliant track career for Hayes, whose mother is a domestic and father a paraplegic as a result of wounds suffered in World War II. In addition to winning two gold medals in Tokyo, Hayes held the world record for the 100-yard dash (9.1), the 60-yard dash (5.9), and the 70-yard dash (6.9).

Yet Hayes's mother doesn't recall Bob exhibiting any of that record speed around the house.

"It would take him two hours to wash dishes," she recalls. "He was the slowest moving boy doing any kind of work around the house. Although he moped doing things around the house, he'd always run when you sent him on an errand. He'd run to and from the grocery store—six blocks. Always ran no matter where I'd send him."

Hayes also took to running because the guys in his neighborhood on Jacksonville's East Side held frequent foot races—and wagered a hefty ten cents on the outcome. Hayes, who won all-state in football, track, basketball, and baseball, usually defeated the others.

Hayes was the youngest of three children, and his older brother, Ernest, outran him when he was young. "That was when I was little," Bob says. "After I had clocked a 9.6 hundred-yard dash at Florida A&M, Ernest still thought he was the bird dog. I came home and we raced. He never asked to run against me again."

With success on the track came the stories.

One rumor had it that Hayes would stride into the dressing room before each meet and ask, "Who's going to be second?" Another alleges that Hayes led the field by such a large margin in one race that he finished running, walked over to the sidelines, and began appraising other runners as they came in. "See that boy there," he would say pointing, "he's pretty good. See the other one. He's going to be alright . . ."

Hayes denies the stories.

Far from being pert, Gaither says Hayes was an easy-going person who just wanted to be one of the boys. More-over, Gaither says Bob liked football better than track.

"He required guidance, but with a boy like Bob, the main thing you have to do is keep him in condition," Jake says. "He did not injure easily. The whole time he was here I remember him having one pulled muscle. He's not a hard boy to coach. His love is football; track was incidental to Bob. If he had a choice between football and track, he'd throw his track shoes out the window. He could hardly wait to get back from the Olympics to get back to football.

"I got criticized for letting him play football, but I couldn't have stopped him if I wanted to. I knew he couldn't make a dime out of track, but with his ability and desire, I knew he'd be tremendous in professional football. After I've had a boy four years, I'm ready for him to start making some money. We used him sparingly because we had so many good athletes in those days." Jake used Hayes as a wide receiver, but says Bob could also punt 40 or 50 yards. But Gaither was cognizant that an injury would have prevented Hayes from competing in the 1964 Olympics. "I wouldn't let him kick because had he gotten hurt, I would have been Mr. Mud himself, the man who ruined our Olympic star," he says.

Hayes, not Gaither, almost ruined the sprinter's life. Bob was placed on academic probation at FAMU, forcing Gaither to cancel some of his meets, including the 1963 Pan American Game in São Paulo, Brazil. "I've got to shock this boy into reality," Gaither said at the time. "He must get his education and be prepared to step out into the world. He should represent the United States in next

Fire and brimstone.

J. Leviton—Atlanta

Gaither casting a watchful eye.

Jake (standing to the extreme right on second row) in a 1926 Knoxville College team photo.

Gaither listening to
Quarterback Ted
Richardson offer game
strategy.

FAMU photo

Jake with what he considers the best one-two running combination in
Florida A&M's history, Al Frazier (left) and Willie Galimore.

FAMU photo

A pensive portrait.

Kneeling, left to right, Robert Mungen and Edward Oglesby; standing, left to right, Costa Kittles, Hansel Tookes, and Bobby Lang; top of ladder, Jake Gaither, and second from top, Robert P. Griffin.

Below: Watchful eyes.

Bob Hayes, knock-kneed and pigeon-toed, could also punt.

Top right: Oakland Raider Defensive End Carleton Oats, a FAMU grad, crashing ball to ground after scoring on a fumble recovery. Meanwhile, Buffalo Bill Quarterback Jack Kemp tries to discover what hit him.

Right: Hewritt Dixon, another of Gaither's products, running for a 69-yard touchdown in the 1967 AFL Championship game.

The Papa Rattler and his offspring.

year's Olympics. But he's got to stay in school to do that."
Hayes did get his academic probation lifted and later was
a double gold-medal winner in the Olympics.

Three years earlier, another incident threatened to
change his life in a way that a track meet could not begin
to match.

On December 3, 1960, Hayes, then a freshman, and
another student, James W. Vickers, eighteen years old,
robbed another student, Frank Barnum, of eleven cents,
two sticks of chewing gum, and two billfolds. Leon
County (Fla.) Probation Department records contain the
account:

On that December day, Hayes and/or Vickers—depending on whose version you believe—decided to rob
Barnum. Vickers began kicking the victim until a police
car, lights flashing and sirens wailing, appeared on the
scene. Vickers was apprehended, but Hayes ran and was
not picked up until the next day. After four days in jail
Hayes signed a confession. Vickers was later given a
prison sentence because he had a previous conviction;
Hayes was given a ten-year probation and placed in the
custody of Jake Gaither. Hayes's story is that he stopped
to tie his shoes and Vickers walked ahead. Before he knew
what was happening, Hayes says, Vickers was holding up
the student with a toy pistol. Hayes said he became fright-
ened and fled when police appeared on the scene.

"I became a part of Jake Gaither," Hayes says now.
"You know he doesn't have any kids and Jakie just took
me in when I got in trouble. I went to jail and he got me
out on parole for an incident I didn't have anything to do
with. It just happened at the time and I ran away. If I

hadn't run, I wouldn't have been in that predicament. Jakie stuck by me all the way. Since that incident, he has stuck by me even more."

Initially, several assistant coaches learned of the incident and brought it to Jake's attention. Gaither's response then was that since Hayes, whom he really didn't know at the time, was beginning his college career in such grand fashion, it might be best just to let him stay in jail. But his view changed when Bob's father asked for Gaither's help.

"I was sitting in the office when his daddy was brought in in his wheel chair," Gaither recalls. "He said, 'I'm Bobby Hayes's daddy.' When they put him in jail, I said let him stay in jail. I didn't know the details, but I said, 'He's a freshman, let him take the punishment for something like that.' I didn't have time to fool with him. So when his father came in, he said, 'Coach, I want you to get my boy out of jail.' Then I began to inquire about what this boy had done and I saw a thing that any kid can get into—he was just in bad company and didn't know it."

On April 11, 1961, Hayes was placed on ten-year probation. While Hayes was achieving status as "the World's Fastest Human," he was reporting to the parole office in Tallahassee. Hayes's arrest remained secret for four years for two reasons: First, Hayes was booked under the name Haynes, instead of Hayes; second, his name was printed in the local newspaper, but it went unnoticed because at the time he had not made his reputation in track. March 12, 1965, the veil of secrecy lifted. Gaither received a long distance telephone call from a reporter with the *Miami Herald*. Gaither usually projects placidity unless he is giving one of his famous pep talks, but his voice rises as he recounts the conversation.

"A newspaperman called me from Miami," Gaither said. "He said, 'I'm preparing an article about that trouble Bob Hayes got into and I want to be sure I get the facts straight.' And when he started asking questions, I said, 'What are you trying to do? Man, this boy has paid his debt. He's been a loyal citizen. The whole state of Florida is proud of his accomplishment—he's got two gold medals. He's just a young kid in school. Why would you want to destroy this boy?' He said, 'Well, these are the facts.' I begged him for thirty or forty minutes."

The story was written, nonetheless. The next day the *Miami Herald* ran the story under the headline "Gold Medal Winner Bob Hayes Outsprints Court Record." With a Tallahassee dateline, the article ran on page 10.

Only Gaither and Hayes had known of the incident and, predictably, there was a vociferous reaction among education officials. Dr. James Carr, chief of academic affairs for the Board of Regents, which operates the state's university system, promised an immediate investigation. FAMU President George W. Gore was in a quandary. He said, "I'm so shocked that I don't know what to say. He's such a gentle boy . . . such a fine boy. If it happened today I would do something about it. But what should I do at this point—four years late? I think Coach Gaither should have told me, but his aim was rehabilitation. In this case, it looks like he did a good job." Normal procedure in such cases was suspension from school.

His voice still loud, Gaither continued: "They called me," he said, referring to the furor. "I said, 'This is a good boy. He made a mistake when he was sixteen years old.

He's been released in my hands and I'll stand by him until hell freezes over.' I said, 'I did it then, I'll do it now, and I'll do it as long as he lives and as long as I live.' It came out in the paper: 'Jake says he'll stand by Bob until hell freezes over'—that was the headline."

Hayes, who had been running in a California meet shortly before the story broke, wrote a nondescript article for Newspaper Enterprise Association (NEA), expressing his feeling about the revelation, but avoiding the question of his complicity:

"When I arrived home I didn't go to practice for about three days. I realized if I had stopped running track, the issue would be dead, for I would be just another American citizen. The story wouldn't be written. But I remembered something Coach Gaither had said in one of his many lectures: 'Basically, people are good. . . .' I prepared myself for this long ago. I decided I would go on. I called my mother, talked to her about it, and before I could tell her my decision she told me to run. She said my friends would understand, that I couldn't let them down.

"I traveled many miles for my country, my state, and my school. I have given advice to many boys. Invariably, my first words are to stay out of trouble and live a clean, healthy life. When I had time to really talk to boys, I would tell them that I have been in trouble and that I was lucky to be where I am today."

Within weeks after the story of Hayes's arrest became known, Gaither, who has always had warm relationships with the state governors, many of them avowed segregationists, telephoned Haydon Burns when it appeared that the parole board was about to recommend against a par-

don of Hayes, and requested a meeting. Gaither says that
after Burns heard Gaither and Bob present their case, he
said, "This boy has had a rope around his neck for three
years. He just returned from the Olympics, where he
represented the state of Florida, his institution, and the
United States government. I don't know how you feel, but
I'm going to take this rope from around this boy's neck
and I hope you agree with me. But whether you do or
whether you don't, he's going to be pardoned. Now how
do you feel?"

One parole official replied, "Mr. Governor, I feel the
same as you do, and I feel sure that the rest of the members of the commission will go along with it. If you'll
recommend a pardon, I'll recommend a pardon."

Burns then turned to Hayes. "Bob, there's just one
thing I'm asking of you," he said. "I want you to autograph
your picture for my boy." Both Gaither and Hayes promised that the picture would be forthcoming in days. "I
remember one thing he said when I got him out," Gaither
says. "He said, 'Coach, there's one thing you will never
have to worry about—I'm never going to get into any
more trouble.' He repeated that the other night when he
called me from San Francisco, and that was ten years
ago."

Two months after the story was published, the Florida
Parole Board unanimously lifted Hayes's probation. Bob
was in Chicago preparing for the College All-Star Game
against the defending NFL champion Cleveland Browns
when the ruling was announced. Hayes had a lackluster
game and his team lost, 24–16.

Otto Graham said, "Hayes has good speed, but he has

trouble catching the ball and doesn't have good moves."
Given his poor pronouncements in the past, no one will
ever mistake Otto for Jimmy the Greek. He is as notorious
for his poor judgment of talent—he once said similiar
things about Jimmy Brown, who went on to become the
best fullback in the history of the game—as Howard Co-
sell is for his verbosity.

But Otto Graham was not the only one critical of Bob.

"Bob Hayes, the Olympic sprint champion who hopes
to make it as a flanker with the Dallas Cowboys, had not
been able to decide to run or not with a couple of punts
and a pass," wrote Dan Jenkins in *Sports Illustrated*.
"Which left inconclusive the matter of his ability to catch
the ball. As one pro scout put it, 'He's got 9.1 speed, 12-flat
hands.'"

In view of Hayes's subsequent exploits, it is not unlikely
that the scout who was quoted has since gone the way of
the World Football League.

The Dallas Cowboys, who drafted Bob as a "future" in
his junior year, never doubted his ability. Their scouting
report on Hayes was prophetic: "He can stop, start and
cut on a dime," it says. "He thinks quickly in all situations.
He is the fastest man in the world. He always wants to win
and is accustomed to winning. He has all the physical skills
to play in the NFL."

Gaither negotiated Hayes's three-year contract, which
called for about $100,000 over that period. Cowboy
owner Clint Murchinson, Jr., disclosed that when the
team signed Hayes, the word *Dallas* appeared 191 million times in foreign newspapers and 41.7 billion times in
United States papers. Anyone who'd go to that extent to

collect data must have been impressed.

Even so, Hayes did not shed his track image easily. Many track standouts had received final rites on the gridiron. They learned belatedly that running over people is not the same as running ahead of them. Ray Norton, Frank Budd, and Glen Davis were all track men who tried professional football and failed. On the other hand, a few did make it: ex-Illinois great Buddy Young and former NCAA champ Bob Boyd. Gaither postulates that the only track stars who succeed in pro football are those who played football first.

"We all know he has great speed," said Cowboy quarterback Don Meredith, now a broadcaster and actor, when Hayes signed a contract. "But can he turn the corner?" Hayes did some turning and tossing before he moved into the starting lineup. End coach Red Hickey worked Hayes unusually hard, and it did take several days for Bob to get adjusted to the new system. He and Hickey had the following encounter:

HAYES: Coach, I can't get past that linebacker. He grabs me everytime I try to go past him.

HICKEY: That's the way it is in this game. You gotta dodge him, get around him some way.

HAYES: I can't do it.

HICKEY: You'll do it or I'll send you home.

HAYES: I'll do it.

Hayes has been doing it ever since. Frank Clark, a teammate, stayed after practice to teach Bob how to catch over his shoulders—with thumbs out. In addition to having to learn to catch on the run, Hayes had a habit of leaping for the ball; he had to be persuaded that no one, not even the world's fastest human, could walk on air.

"He has great hands," says Hickey. "And that's something nobody can teach. I guess the best thing about him is that he's tough. He concentrates on the ball, right into his hands. That's where track men let you down. They tend to roll their eyes toward that defensive man coming up on their blind side. It's what we call hearing footsteps. Hayes hasn't heard a footstep yet."

It seems it was the defensive players who heard the footsteps—Bob's.

For example, Dick Lynch of the New York Giants was knocked to the ground by one of Hayes's blocks. "I didn't know you could hit like that," Lynch said. Hayes retorted, "Well, you're lying on the ground, aren't you?"

St. Louis Cardinal safetyman Larry Wilson, after chasing Hayes, said, "I used to wish I was twenty pounds heavier. Now I wish I was twenty miles an hour faster."

"There are just three things you can do with him," said Irv Cross, a former Rams defensive back turned broadcaster. "Jolt him, crowd him out of his route, or just pray."

Even former FAMU players received no special treatment. After leaving New York Giants defensive back Clarence Childs in his tracks, Hayes said, "I wasn't worried about Clarence. I knew him at Florida A&M. He was just a 9.4 man."

In his first two games as a pro, Hayes touched the ball four times and scored on all four, although one was nullified because of a penalty. In his first two weeks, he won all the awards available to a member of the Cowboys. He won the Outstanding Play Award, a game ball, and Outstanding Offensive Player of the Month. He finished the season with 46 receptions for 1,103 yards. His 21.8-yard average on receptions and 12 touchdowns led the league.

"If he never catches a pass, he's worth a couple of touchdowns a game," says former teammate Dan Reeves. Cowboy President Tex Schramm observed, "The remarkable thing about Hayes is that he does something outstanding in every game—something different." Tom Landry, the laconic head coach, says, "Hayes is our game breaker. Even if most teams double-team Bobby, we still have to hit him."

Hayes was traded to the San Francisco 49ers prior to the 1975 season. He had already accomplished more than most receivers in their career. In ten years, he had caught 365 passes for 7,295 yards and scored 76 touchdowns. But the statistic that Hayes is most proud of is being out of jail.

"Jake and I formed a lasting relationship," Hayes says. "I would try to do things around Jake's house because I really thought he did me a favor. I don't feel I can ever repay him. When I became the fastest human in the world, everybody began to look up to Florida A&M more. I had a lot of opportunities to travel around. People would ask me, 'What can I do for you?' and I would tell them to give me a couple of tickets so that I could have who I want here. Coach never had anything like that. On these trips Jake and I got to know each other better—we would stay in the same room and even eat breakfast together. By Jake not having kids of his own, I think he took me in even more. He took me in more as a kid than as an athlete. Jake and I had become close after the incident and I had gotten a bad deal. I've never been a conceited-type guy—I was

Jake's All-American type of guy.

"After I started in pro ball, I got Jake a lot of free trips. When we were training in California, he would come out and then go to Hawaii for a week and then back home. I used to call Jake all the time and would send telegrams to the boys telling them to do it right or not at all. I guess Jake must have said, 'This guy has to have some good in him because of all the boys I've sent into the pros, none of them has ever done this before.' One time I sent Jake a radio and he told everybody. I had to send five or six more. It's not that I'm trying to repay him for what he did on December 3, 1960—it's just my feeling for him."

When Gaither broke his leg November 11, 1967, Hayes was one of the first at his bedside. Gaither suffered the fracture in a game against Southern University. FAMU was leading 13–6 mid-way the second quarter when a Southern player intercepted a Florida A&M pass and began racing along the FAMU sideline. As the player was chased out of bounds, he ran into Jake. "I just froze," Gaither said afterwards. Jake finished coaching the game and did not go into the hospital until the next day to be operated on for the fracture. That Sunday, the Cowboys played the New Orleans Saints in New Orleans. Al Tabor, a former scout for the Saints, now a staff member of the Cleveland Browns, told Hayes that Gaither had been injured the previous night. Bob called Sadie and inquired of Jake's condition, and then Bob called his wife, Altamese, telling her to pack his bags. Hayes flew back to Dallas on the team's charter flight, picked up his luggage, and flew to Tallahassee the same day.

Gaither beamed when Hayes entered his hospital room.

They are very close, for each has meant something special to the other. Gaither has often been accused of showing favoritism toward Hayes, a charge he does not deny. He told Bill McGrotha of the Tallahassee *Democrat,* "You know there are just some boys who tug at your heartstrings more." Obviously Bob Hayes is one of them.

Jake follows the careers of all of his players religiously, but especially Bob Hayes's. Once as he was finishing up a night's driving while on vacation, Jake's big Lincoln Continental came to an abrupt halt. Gaither was listening intently to the Dallas–Green Bay exhibition game, a contest in which the lead changed hands back and forth. Mrs. Gaither observed smoke escaping from the hood. "Jake, Jake, the motor's on fire!" she exclaimed. "Wait just a minute, Sadie," he replied, still listening to the radio. "Bob just scored a touchdown."

7

Split-Line T

Coach Jake Gaither has proven himself to be an offensive genius. His Split-Line T has brought a new dimension to football.

—WOODY HAYES
Head football coach
Ohio State University

The above is heady praise for the coach of a small black college in Florida. But there's more.

"Coach Jake Gaither's Split-Line T is one of the finest offensive innovations to come along in years," according to Bobby Dodd, head football coach at Georgia Tech.

The preceding quotes appear on the jacket of Gaither's book, *The Split-Line T Offense.* In the book, which appeared in 1963, Gaither explains the formation. Now both pro and college teams use the extra-wide line splits, as well as some of the other new tactics Gaither describes in his book. What follows is a capsule summary of the innovative formation.

The Gaither alignment spreads offensive linemen over an area of about 48 feet, as contrasted with a previously more usual distance of about 33 feet from offensive end to offensive end, thus forcing the defense to cover an area at least 15 feet wider than when the offense line up in the regular T-formation (see Figures A and B).

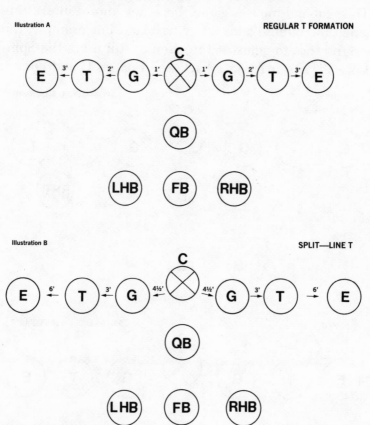

Illustration A   **REGULAR T FORMATION**

Illustration B   **SPLIT—LINE T**

Traditionally, offenses have been dictated by the defensive alignment—if the defensive linemen played wide, the offensive sent its backs up the middle; if the defense crowded the center, the backs would go outside. The major advantage of the Split-Line T is that it, not the defense, dictates team positioning. Defensive players must go where the offensive players are or become vulnerable. This cat-and-mouse game becomes more interesting when the offense adds a few wrinkles. For example, the defense has to adjust if the offense, still using the Split-Line T, slots or flanks a back (see Figures C and D).

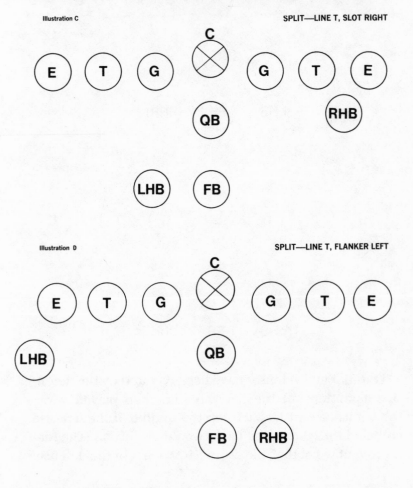

Illustration C   SPLIT—LINE T, SLOT RIGHT

Illustration D   SPLIT—LINE T, FLANKER LEFT

To add further intrigue, the offense—either with the backs in the normal positions or flanked—can go to an unbalanced line, forcing the defense to adapt again.

Gaither says the wider line spacing, in addition to applying pressure on the defense, provides better blocking angles for offensive linemen. The backs do not suffer under this arrangement, because they remain in the same positions they were in in the conventional T, from 4 to 4½ yards behind the line.

If the defense tries to compensate, say, by shifting an extra lineman to one side of the center, the quarterback should be able to recognize this manuever and call an audible (a play change made at the line of scrimmage) to take advantage of the player being out of position. Nothing forces a defense to stop experimenting quicker than a 25-yard run over a spot just vacated by a shifted defensive player.

Gaither's book also describes two other novel techniques. In the first, the linemen stand with one foot slightly behind the other and, in the second, the linemen line up on the heels of the center rather than even with the football. Both provide advantages when blocking.

Florida A&M achieved phenomenal success while using the unconventional Split-Line T. FAMU won 62 games and lost 5 from 1956 through 1962. It is difficult to discern exactly how successful Gaither's teams were by reading his book, however. The book's jacket says FAMU averaged 41.7 points per game; in the preface, Gaither says they averaged 41.8 points a game; and in the first chapter, he says his teams averaged 41.9

points over the same seven-year period.

All of the figures are incorrect.

FAMU's records show that during the seven-year period in question, the Rattlers scored 2,848 points in 67 games, which averages out to 42.50 points. Gaither apparently got his last figure (who knows where he got the other two) when he, after listing each year's scoring *average*—the sum of which comes to 293.50—proceeded to average the averages, which would have given him 41.92. However, as any student of Math 101 knows, one doesn't average averages, only numbers.

And as any student of Florida A&M football will tell you, to contend that the university was successful because of the Split-Line T is preposterous, to say the least. It was simply a matter of FAMU having a monopoly on the state's black football talent. Some athletes had been All-Conference or All-State in high school, yet when they enrolled in Florida A&M, the only time they got off the bench was when the band played the National Anthem.

Rumor has it that one opponent was so awe-struck that when FAMU left the field prematurely at the end of one game, the opposing team, still bedazzled, ran three plays and kicked a field goal—which was wide.

Gaither says his high-voltage 1961 team was probably his best, although he is prouder of his 1969 team, the one that defeated the University of Tampa in the state's first interracial collegiate football game. The American Football Coaches Association named Gaither small college Coach of the Year in January 1962, after his '61 team went undefeated, outscoring its opponents 506 to 33. The obituary list reads as follows:

Benedict	52–0
Lincoln	49–6
Morris Brown	56–0
Bethune-Cookman	76–0
South Carolina State	60–0
N.C. A&T	34–12
Allen	71–0
Southern	46–0
Texas Southern	48–7
Jackson State	14–8

That talent-laden juggernaut had five backs who could run the 100-yard dash in 10 seconds or less, and three tackles who weighed more than 260 pounds; yet none of them were starters. The players included Bob Hayes, who sat on the bench; Al Denson, later a league-leading wide receiver for the Denver Broncos; Robert Paremore, a 9.4 halfback who was later a journeyman in the pros; Curtis Miranda, a center drafted by the New York Giants; Walt Highsmith, subsequently a lineman for the Continental Football League; Carleton Oats, who became starting defensive tackle for the Oakland Raiders; Bobby Felts, later a running back for the Detroit Lions; and Hewritt Dixon, who was afterwards All-Pro fullback for the Oakland Raiders.

After FAMU had annihilated its opponents by such large scores, Gaither called a team meeting to caution against overconfidence. John Underwood of *Sports Illustrated* gave the following account:

"Mid-way in the season Coach Jake Gaither of Florida A&M University gathered his players in the dressing room to warn them that unbeaten teams, like expensive china, are always one slip away from the broom and dust-pan. 'Beware,' he said. 'There is a law of averages.' From the circle of squad members, a senatorial type clattered to his feet and spoke. 'No, sir,' he said. 'We *repealed* that law.' "

Evidently they had.

But some coaches think that Jake should repeal or at least amend his unwritten rule that allows his teams to run up scores. He has been criticized, not unduly, for not calling off his squad after it becomes clear that the other team has no chance of winning the game. Gaither's men don't just vanquish the opposition, they humiliate it mer-cilessly, piling score on top of score.

Is all that necessary? Can't you build up a considerable lead and allow your subs to play the remainder of the game?

Gaither rationalizes. "I don't like to run up a score," he says unpersuasively. "But you can't tell the boys not to block or tackle or run or score if they can. If you tell a team you want them to play hard, you can't turn around and pull punches."

Other coaches, however, manage to defeat their oppo-nents soundly without emasculating them. Football, after all, is supposed to be a game, not a massacre. Gaither's explanation has a hollow ring when one examines the record. His 1961 team was leading South Carolina State 44–0 going into the final quarter—hardly a chance for South Carolina State to stage a comeback. Yet FAMU scored another 16 points to make the score 60–0. In the game against Bethune-Cookman, the Rattlers led 62–0 entering the fourth quarter. Final score: FAMU 76, Bethune-Cookman 0. It seems that each game was an attempt to break the collegiate scoring record set by Georgia Tech on October 7, 1916. In that game, Tech defeated Cumberland College 222–0.

FAMU was particularly devastating back in the early 1960s when they were playing platoon football, the act of substituting an entire unit rather than individual players. Jake encouraged competition between the units and, like other schools, gave each their own identity. *Sports Illustrated,* in its October 8, 1962 issue, noted:

"Tom Nugent of Maryland calls his first, second and third teams the M-squad, the Hustlers and the Gangbusters. Marvin Bass at South Carolina has the Warhorses, the Bushwhackers and the Stonewalls. But the coach who has conjured up the most vivid image of the football player (for the football players, anyway) is none of these. He is Jake Gaither of Florida A&M who calls the three teams on his 60-man squad Blood, Sweat and Tears."

From time to time, however, injuries necessitated mixing a little blood with sweat and sweat with tears.

Former FAMU halfback Clarence Childs has a different interpretation of Florida A&M's three-platoon system. "We had one to play offense," he explains, "one to play defense, and one to go to classes."

8

God of the Rattlers

"I remember the time we were playing North Carolina A and T and we were behind by seven points," says Al Frazier, a former Rattler who now lives in New York. "I think we had twenty-five seconds left in the game. We were back in our own territory, and I think there was time for two more plays. At that particular time, my tooth had come through my lip, my mouth was swollen, and I had played the whole game without sitting on the sideline—I was just pooped. As soon as I came out of the game for one play, Jake came over and just looked at me, knowing that I didn't want to go back into the game. I kind of looked off a bit and he said, 'Hell, baby, how are you feeling?'

"All this blood was running down my face, my mouth was puffed out and he says, 'How are you feeling?' I looked at him and said, 'I'm okay.' He said, 'Go back in there and flank out and tell Jefferson to throw you the pass.' I went into the ball game, gave Jefferson the play, flanked out on the end and ran a pretty good pattern. I looked up and the ball was there—it hit me right in the hands. From there on, I took it in for about sixty yards and we won the ball game. Jake came over later, and I told

him I really hadn't felt like going in but that I'd do anything for him. Since Jake asked, I had to go back in and
try again."

Frazier's experience amply demonstrates what is perhaps Gaither's greatest attribute—his ability to motivate
people. In addition to his actual football knowledge,
which is considerable, Jake knows how to excite a player.
When he asks players to jump, they don't ask, "How
come?" They ask, "How high?" When he tells them to run
through a brick wall, they don't ask why, only which one.
If Gaither asked them to walk to hell, they'd start packing.

"I'm a high-strung coach," says Hansel E. Tookes, a
long-time Gaither assistant and present athletic director
at FAMU. "Even after playing four years under the guy
and working with him for twenty-five years, when he
gave his pregame talk, I'd start snorting and biting—let's
get going. I think football is a game of emotion, and this
was Jake's greatest contribution, not his X's and O's. I
know there are some shortcomings in Jake, but he's got
that first thing—the ability to motivate. This is why Jake
has been able to get away with a lot of stuff, because the
guy was so motivated to *want* to win. I know many
coaches who are great in techniques, execution, and
know-how. This man was great in the thing I think is most
important—making a guy have a burning desire to *want*
to win."

Gaither usually got his message across gently, calling
everyone "baby," or "honey."

"There was no screaming," recalls Frazier. "He was not
emotional in that sense. However, you could see the expression on his face when you upset him. He'd say, 'Hell,

baby, what are you doing now? Get back in there.' It was a positive approach. If you were half-way decent, you'd feel badly because you blew the play."

Bob Hayes explains, "You're around him so much that a mistake is just a mistake—a mild error as he calls it. He won't snatch you out of a ball game because you made a mistake. He came to Dallas one time on my birthday and I scored four touchdowns. There hasn't been one football game except one championship game that he has been there and I didn't score a touchdown. Jake is so influential on me, that when he's around, I explode. There is something natural about the man that can move people. A lot of people can't move me."

There are some players who can't move at all—or at least not in the right direction.

One time a halfback forgot his blocking assignment and ran the wrong direction. Giving one of his harsher tongue-lashings, Jake said, "Baby, have you got a playbook? When you eat, take it with you. When you go to the toilet, take it with you. When you go to see your girl, take it with you."

Another time, Hubert Ginn, now with the Miami Dolphins, was subjected to Gaither's criticism. Ginn, a star halfback, had been avoiding running wind sprints by missing the first fifteen minutes of practice. Jake called the players together at the end of one session. As Gaither tells it, "I said, 'Now, Mr. Ginn, I want you to help me. I want you to help me be fair to my boys. I want to be fair to all my boys. Will you help me?' He said, 'Yes sir, Coach.' I said, 'Mr. Ginn, we practice at four o'clock. John Jones over there comes at four o'clock; James Brown comes at four o'clock; Charlie Smith comes at four o'clock, but you come at four-fifteen. How can I be fair to the rest of these boys if I permit you to come in here fifteen minutes late every day?' I said, 'I want to be fair to all my boys. Will you help me do that?' He said, "Yes sir, Coach.' I said, 'Practice is at four o'clock every day—for *all* of my boys.' I had no more trouble with Mr. Ginn."

Gaither also used psychology effectively.

"One time a boy came into my office to see me about chewing him out," he says. "I said, 'I'm on you because I see potential in you. I'm trying to get you ready for the game.' He asked why I didn't chew out John Jones and I said, 'I've just about forgotten about John Jones.' I said, 'Don't worry when I chew you out, worry when I don't say anything to you.' He said, 'Coach, you can chew me out as long as you want to. Just chew me out.' "

Jake continues to amplify on how he motivates players:

"Kindness is the universal language that all people understand. I made it a habit to never leave the field with a boy feeling that I was mad at him. Before I left the field, I'd pat him on the shoulder and say, 'Don't think I got anything against you. I'm chewing you out for your own good. You're still my boy.' That means a lot to that kid. If you don't do something like that to the boy, when he comes to practice the next day, he's got a chip on his shoulder—he figures Coach is mad at him and he's still in the doghouse. He'll sulk and you won't get the best work out of him. But if you let him know that you'll forgive him —just don't make that mistake again—the guy will come back with plenty of enthusiasm, believing 'I'm still Coach's boy.' They want to be in the good graces of the coach; they don't want to be in the doghouse."

Gaither didn't like to have his players in a girlfriend's doghouse, either.

"One thing I insisted of the girls," Jake says, grinning sheepishly. "No problem on Saturday. Hold the problems until Sunday. On game day, I want my boys happy." It didn't always work out that way, as Mrs. Gaither will attest.

"A canceled check came through for five dollars, and on the corner was marked 'candy,' " Sadie recalls. "I saw red. When he came home, I was cool toward him. He said, 'What the heck is wrong with you?' I said, 'I went over the canceled checks.' He said, 'So what? You handled them, I didn't.' I said, 'There's one check I don't understand and you wrote it.' He said, 'What is it?' I said, 'You have a check there for candy. What's that for?' There was a minute of quietness. He said, 'My quarterback is having trouble with his girl, and I couldn't get my plays to go. His mind is on something else. I went down there and bought the biggest box of candy that I could find. I gave it to him to give to that girl. And he started playing football.' "

Still another reason Jake gets along with and motivates people is because he can captivate them. He has the ability to make people laugh; it comes easily. He embellishes stories, always giving vivid details and demonstrating his flair for the dramatic, thus creating bedlam among his listeners. His favorite, predictably enough, concerns the time he was in Chicago attending a meeting of the American Football Coaches Association, of which he is a permanent trustee.

As Jake tells it, the coaches were standing in the lobby

of the Conrad Hilton Hotel, exchanging tales, drinking, and looking at the guests passing through the lobby, especially the curvaceous women. The weather was wretched. It had rained for several days before and now was freezing and snowing heavily. A taxi driver and his customer entered the lobby while the coaches were downstairs; the driver approached the cashier to make change for his passenger. After getting change for $5, the driver put $2.50 in his pocket for the ride and gave the remainder to the rider. After pausing diplomatically for several minutes, hoping to receive a tip, the driver slowly began moving away once it appeared that no tip would be forthcoming.

"Just a minute, just a minute," the passenger yelled to the driver. "Don't you want your tip?" The color in the driver's face changed from lifeless pale to a warm red. But that lasted only until he received his tip—four cents. The driver gave the rider a vexed glance and turned to go back to his taxi. The customer, sensing the driver's displeasure, asked, "What's the matter? Don't you like your tip?" The driver carefully masked his true feelings and in his best manner replied, "Yes, I like my tip. But I was wondering if you'd let me tell your fortune." The customer, delighted that the driver was not upset, said, "Go ahead and tell my fortune. I have nothing to hide—my life is an open book."

The taxi driver was seemingly as excited as the customer now; he couldn't wait to begin. "Okay, this first penny tells me that you're a Scotsman," he said, pausing for confirmation. "Yes, I'm a Scotsman," the passenger said ostentatiously. "I'm a Scotsman, but how in the world did you know that?" The driver drawled, "Oh, you'd have to be a Scotsman to be out on a night like this." He continued: "Now, this second penny tells me that you're a Catholic." Amused, the passenger asked, "How in the world did you know that?" The driver replied, "Oh, you'd have to have the faith of a Catholic to be out on a night like this." The rider marveled at the remarkable taxi driver. "Now this third penny tells me that you're a bachelor," the driver said, still impressing his fare. "Fellow," the passenger said, almost ready to concede that the driver was indeed gifted with special powers. "How did you know that?" The driver answered, "Oh, I know all about you. I'm a fortune teller . . . Now this fourth penny," he said, pausing momentarily, "tells me that your father was also a bachelor."

Gaither usually gets a good reaction to that one.

He also likes to tell another joke.

A few years ago, as Gaither tells it, Florida A&M's football team was playing Grambling State University in Tallahassee. Jake paced furiously up and down the sidelines. His team, trailing by 4 points, had just returned a punt to midfield. It would be the team's last opportunity to win.

Gaither sent in a play calling for the quarterback to pass to his right end about 15 yards downfield. Two drunks were sitting in the stands next to Gaither's wife. After the first play was completed successfully, one turned to the other and said, "You know, that's the same play I would have called. The ssaaaaammme play." The second play Gaither sent in was a draw to the fullback, which picked up 20 yards, down to the 15-yard line. The same drunk yelled, "That's it! That's it! That's the same play I would have called, tha, tha, tha . . . same play." Still another pass, this time to the left halfback, moved the team 13 yards closer to the goal line. It was fourth down for Florida at the 2-yard line—the last play of the game. Mrs. Gaither, who had been sitting silently, if uncomfortably, throughout those final minutes, turned to the drunk and said, "You've been talking all day. Now what would you call now?" The drunk, without batting an eye, replied, "Hell, I've gotten them this far, let Jake take over now."

Jake does take over, even when he's off the field. For instance, he would often pass a group of male students on campus and say, "Gentlemen, gentlemen." Then after taking a few steps, he would pivot, and add, "Now if I made a mistake, I apologize." To which the students would reply unhesitatingly, "You didn't make a mistake, Coach. No, sir, I'm a gentleman, I'm a gentleman."

"I do that regardless of where I am or what they look like," Gaither explains. "I say, 'Gentlemen'—everybody respects that. They say, 'Here's a coach who recognizes me as a gentleman.' There's a little ego [Jake pronounces it egg-o] in everybody—they want respect. There is a sacredness in everybody's personality and they're entitled to respect. People don't like to be looked down on. They like to feel they're somebody, too. That's the way God intended us to feel—that's why He made man above beast."

This is not to say that Jake does not want his players to act beastly on the field—he does.

"I want my boys to be *ag*-ile, *mo*-bile and *hos*-tile," he says, accenting the first syllable of each word. "I tell our boys we can't use clumsy guys who fall over their feet. I've sent them to dance classes to help their coordination. That's what I mean by *ag*-ile. I use the word *mo*-bile for quickness. I once had a backfield with a 9.1, a 9.3, and a 9.4 runner. We'd like to hit the hole on a quick handoff in eight-tenths of a second. A daredevil who doesn't worry about getting hurt is my idea of hostility. I don't like any good-natured football players. We don't want anybody running over others and then apologizing. Mow him down, then stand over him and yell, 'I'll eat you up.' Make him wish he had never been born."

Jake knew how to get his players at their emotional peak; he was the master of the pregame pep talk, knowing when to turn the electricity up and when to turn it down.

"He could get you up for the game even if you came into the dressing room feeling a little low," says Al Frazier. "When he finished, we'd break out of that dressing room and I guess if we had seen some of the opposition at that moment, we would have tackled them right there."

Gaither says, "A lot of coaches disagree, but I believe in the old-time pep talk. I belong to the school of Knute Rockne." He says he does not rehearse pep talks; he doesn't know what he will say until the words actually come out of his mouth.

Gaither says he first observed how emotions can be used to make humans surpass what they envision as their capability by watching his father deliver his Sunday morning sermons. Jake, then just a child, witnessed persons entering the church leaning on canes, with stooped backs, and hardly able to move. But once Rev. Gaither began his antics—shouting, flailing his hands, and praising the Lord—those same church members would toss away their canes, walk upright, and dance in the aisles. Then once the service was over, they'd return to their former state and struggle back out the door.

There was another experience that happened when Jake was coaching in high school that proved to be didatic in this respect.

"There was a fire in one of the buildings one night, and we all rushed in to save the papers," he says. "There was a heavy safe in the building and in the excitement, three of us picked up that safe and dumped it out of a window. The next morning when the fire was over, it took five people just to *tilt* that safe. I never forgot that; it showed me how much a person can do in the excitement of the moment."

However, not all of Jake's pep talks were in the fire-and-brimstone mold. He also knew how to use the soft touch.

One year, with his team trailing Bethune-Cookman College 20–19 at the half, thanks to an arm-tackling defense and an impotent offense, Gaither went into the dressing room and said, "Well, I found out one thing I didn't know . . . I didn't know I was coaching a bunch of sissies." With that pronouncement, he spun on the toe of his right foot and the heel of his left and walked out of the room. FAMU returned the second-half kickoff 80 yards for a touchdown and won the game by four touchdowns.

"Coach would always cry those crocodile tears," says Purcell Houston, a former quarterback. "We knew he put onions in his handkerchief just so he could cry in front of us." He also would make a point of speaking to each player individually. "Ginn, we're depending on you tonight," he'd say. "Thomas, give me all ya got . . . Evans, we may have to throw a little more, so be ready . . . Harris, reach back into that pocket and give me something extra . . ."

Gaither contends that prayer, not his evangelical pep talks, were what motivated his players.

"The most inspirational effect on my players can be secured by prayer," he says. "I think that all my boys are inspired by prayer more than anything else. I never realized that until fifteen years later when some of them told me. They wouldn't go on the field unless we prayed. I made that mistake one time in Atlanta against Morris Brown. We were leading by about twenty-five or thirty points at the halftime. We were all feeling good. I said, 'Well, boys, it's about time for us to go back. Everybody out.' Not a single man moved. The captain walked over to me and said, 'Coach, haven't you forgotten something?' I said, 'Yes, I'm sorry. I apologize.' And I apologized to the kids. They wouldn't move until I said a prayer for them. If football at this school—at least while I was coaching— has done no more than given our players a belief in prayer, a faith in God, it's done its job. I want every player that played for me to have faith in the Old Man upstairs. I can do no more for a boy's character than to give him the faith and beliefs in a power that is stronger than he. I tell them, 'Put your hand in the hand of the Man from Galilee.' To me, that's been a part of my coaching from nineteen twenty-seven, when I started, to when I finished in nineteen sixty-nine. Religion is the dominant part of my life."

But even Jake's religious fervor is spiced. He usually

begins each team prayer with, "O, God of the Rattlers [he says it's okay to call the Lord 'God of the Rattlers' because he is God of everything], we are here before you again, dear Father, in another contest. Please give these boys the will and the power to exemplify on the field what we have been trying to teach them. Help them play hard. Dear Father, we're not asking for victory, but only that the best team wins." Jake's players say Gaither is sincere with his prayers, but he always seems to remind the Lord that Florida A&M is really the best team.

In the past, quite a few FAMU players were highly emotional and therefore needed little prodding by Gaither. For instance, the tradition of shouting "Hubba, Hubba" as a substitute for saying Amen was begun in the 1950s by a player called Hubba Brock. Brock had served in the Hubba, Hubba unit in the Army, and he carried the tradition over to football. When he was sent into a game, he would shout, "Hubba, Hubba" before sprinting onto the field. As he left the field, he would again shout, "Hubba, Hubba" and leave the field full-speed; he would slide baseball fashion out-of-bounds or throw a cross-body block in the air. One time Brock threw his body into mid-air as he was exiting from the field and landed on Gaither while yelling, "Hubba, Hubba." Jake looked at Brock and said tersely, "Hubba Hell." Yet Gaither never curtailed Brock's antics.

Another player, a center, had a habit of goose stepping as he left the huddle, pointing downfield toward the opposition. After he graduated the alumni wanted his successor to do likewise, but Gaither never insisted, saying each player should be allowed to be himself.

Through the use of pep talks and psychology and with dedication, Jake Gaither worked toward one goal: perfection. He calls it "The Spirit of Excellence," a phrase used to describe his obsession with doing his best and persuading his players to do likewise.

"There is no place in the life of my people for mediocre performances," he lectures. "We must excel. Some of the Chicago people were amazed at Galimore's desire when he got there. They asked me, 'Coach, why does your boy run so hard?' and I told them this: 'For a black boy, this is not just a game of football. He is carrying a cross of fifteen million blacks on his shoulders. Willie Mays was a great baseball player because fifteen million people said, 'Willie, you represent us.' Joe Louis was great for the same reason. This has to be the dominating factor in the life of any black. There is no place in our life for mediocrity. If your job is to sweep this room, I want you to sweep it the best you can. If you're a dentist, I want you to be able to pull teeth better than any other dentist in your community.''

Gaither's deep baritone voice grows deeper and slower as he says, "We try to evaluate our boys, not by the number of games they win, not by how good a football player they are, but on how each will do ten or fifteen years later. Take Al Denson," he says, referring to the former Denver Broncos wide receiver. "He bought a beautiful home in Jacksonville. He had two filling stations down there. When his days ended in professional football, he had his feet solidly on the ground. I feel proud of him. I feel proud of Hewritt Dixon, too. We got doctors, we got lawyers, we got principals, we got probation officers, we got boys with doctorate degrees, we got presidents of colleges . . . The greatest joy that comes to me is seeing that a boy does well in life. He could be a helluva athlete, but you could run across him in four or five years and he could be a drunkard or have a lousy reputation in his community and I wouldn't be proud of him. He played football and that's about all I could say about him. So, the joy is that it means a whole lot if you can feel that you've been partly responsible for a boy being where he is."

But on the football field, as in life, Gaither wants his players to win.

Jake recalls, "One person said, 'All you worry about is winning.' I said, 'What else do you want me to think about? I'm a coach. Yeah, I want to win.' I don't see how anyone can coach conscientiously in competitive sports without setting as his goal the winning of the ball game. But I think along the way to winning you can establish certain basic fundamentals that are necessary for winning: It's hard work, it's dedication to the cause, it's giving attention to instructions, it's following the orders of your coach, it's obeying the play calling of the quarterback, it's working in harmony with your teammates, it's unselfish devotion to duty—all of these have to be put together. Those are the character traits that we want to develop in a boy while we're moving toward the accomplishment of our final goal of winning.

"By the same token, we make it clear to the boys that you can expect to lose sometimes, but a loss can be a stepping stone to a victory if it's utilized in the right way." Jake emphasizes that losing *can* be a stepping stone, but he leaves the distinct impression that, given the choice, he'd much rather win. "Football is so close to life," he says. "You can't win all the time. There are going to be the times when you lose your loved one, you lose your job, you can't balance your budget, a baby is sick, a friend lets you down—those are reverses. But the measure of a man is how well he can come back—how well he can correct the mistake that put him in that position in the first place."

He continues, "They talk about building character. If building character means losing, then I don't want anything to do with it. I can build more character winning than any man can losing. It's fourth down and goal to go at the two. We are going to run off tackle. I want that defensive tackle double-teamed. I want that halfback to kick out on the corner back. And I want my fullback to take the football and charge with his knees under his chin —I want him to run up that linebacker's stomach and leave him flat. Now, you tell me that you're going to talk about character to that poor linebacker?"

Although all coaches, as far as can be determined, would rather win—some will even try to build character along the way—they tend to differ on how best to achieve this goal; some have different methods, yet produce the same result. Many feel that it is the compilation of little things that contributes to a final victory.

"First go out and get yourself a couple of strong two-hundred-sixty-pounders," advices Bob Blackman, head football coach at Cornell University. "It doesn't matter if they can block or tackle, or even run, because what you want them for is to put you on their shoulders and carry you off the field after games. When the alumni sees that they'll say, 'He may not be much of a coach, but at least the boys like him.' "

Jake had his techniques, too.

"I would always sing the blues," he says. "It's bad coaching to blame your boys for losing a ball game, even though it may be true. The public doesn't like it and the public —nine times out of ten—is sympathetic toward the players. If you begin to make excuses for losing the ball game and putting it on your boys, you're making an enemy. The safest thing to do is take the blame. Bear Bryant does it all the time. It's probably true that coaches lose games. If we [the team] lose, there are certain things I failed to do: I didn't get my boys up for the game. I didn't properly prepare them. I ignored some things I shouldn't have ignored. I always sang the blues and I did it on purpose. Regardless of what I had at the beginning of the season, I'd say, 'Well, we got a tough job, we lost so many key men, we got inexperienced kids, we just hope we can win more than we lose.'

"Alright, as the season goes along and we win the first game, they say, 'He must have done a helluva job. He told us he didn't have anything to start with.' You win the second game and they say, 'You know, that guy is a helluva coach out there. He started with nothing.' And if you have a good season, they'll say, 'Man, he did a helluva job.' If you lose a game, they say, 'Coach told you out front not to expect too much.' Ain't no way in the world you can lose. If you sing the blues and then have a good season, you're a helluva coach. If you sing the blues and have a bad season, you're an honest coach—'He told you out front.' Sing the blues all the time, but don't sing them to your boys. I tell them, 'Don't pay attention to what I say in the papers. I believe we got one of the greatest teams we've ever had. We got potential. Let's lull them to sleep. I want you to surprise them. We got a great team; I believe in you. You can never lose by singing the blues and it's hard to get coaches to see it."

There was also Jake's willingness to involve his assistant coaches in the decision-making process.

Although Jake's reliance on his assistants began when he was recovering from the brain operation, he continued the practice throughout his career. For example, the end coach would be responsible for all the ends, both on the field and in the classrooms. Similarly, the tackle coach and other assistants had areas of responsibility. And before each game, the assistant coach assigned to handle certain positions, not Jake, would decide who would start. During game situations when a position appeared weak, Gaither would tell the appropriate coach and that coach would make his own substitution. Consequently the assistant coaches felt they were in a position of responsibility—and they were held accountable.

"I reasoned this way," explains Gaither. "The men who coached these boys every day knew them better than I did. They practiced with them and they knew who the best blockers were and who the best tacklers were, so I delegated that responsibility. If they had any ideas, we'd try them. When the game was over, I'd say, 'Your ends played a very good game.' And I'd tell the sportswriters. I'd give them all the credit to the extent that when the writers asked, 'What do you do, Coach?' I'd say, 'I just organize. Just give me credit for selecting good assistants.' "

Hansel Tookes explains how this affected the assistant coaches.

"One thing I always admired about Jake was that he gave me complete command of developing those players that I was supposed to develop," he says. "I let him know who was ready. He'd let me make that decision. He made me feel I was important—what I did was right and my decisions were right. We had our ups and downs, but basically he was a good administrator. He respected your judgment. When I made my selections, I worked like hell to prove to Jake that this was the right selection even if I had to take him home with me, feed him, run him, work with him in the summertime. I had made the selection that this boy was for him, even though Jake may have thought otherwise. But had he said, 'This man had the background, more potential—play this man—inwardly, you know, I wouldn't have put forth the same amount of energy into developing somebody else's selection that I would my own. That's human nature."

Gaither was also considerate of his players.

"I don't try to single out boys for their mistakes," he says. "They feel bad enough about it without my having to reemphasize it. We also try not to yank a boy out immediately following a mistake. We prefer to let him stay in the game a little longer and make the substitution when it's not noticeable. We have no desire to embarrass that boy because he made a mistake. We realize that he wants to win the game as much as any coach on the bench or fan in the stand. He didn't make that mistake on purpose. He probably dropped that touchdown pass because he couldn't help it."

Of course, Gaither has traditionally gotten the highly motivated player, not what some coaches now refer to as "the new athlete."

"I've been used to dealing with a hungry boy," he says. "I don't mean hungry just for food in his tummy, but he's hungry for recognition. He's hungry for satisfying his ego. He's hungry for being wanted and wants to be *somebody*. That's the kind of kid I have been accustomed to dealing with. And I tell that boy, 'Hold your shoulders back, look the world square in the eye, and get that shuffle out of your feet. Feel that God gave you the potential to do a good job. Ask no quarter, give no quarter. Say to the world that God gave you great potential to do His job with excellence.' We want our boys to be saturated with a burning desire to excel . . . to win . . . to be on top. To satisfy that hunger that's there."

One of those hungry boys, as Jake calls them, complained of the temperature, which had soared past ninety degrees. "Coach, this sun is hot," the player said. Gaither replied, "Yes, my boy, that sun is hot. I've been trying to think of a way to put an umbrella over that sun just for you. If you can practice and play under this Florida sun, you can play under anybody's sun. You ain't gonna dream no number, you ain't gonna win no Irish Sweepstakes. You gonna have to work for everything you get."

But not all players under Gaither worked for *everything* they got, some have gotten special treatment. Gaither has often turned his head when his star players break his rules, and he admits as much.

"You find yourself in situations where you have to compromise," he says. "The world operates on compromise.

You don't want to compromise a principle, but if through patience, perseverence, tolerance, and understanding you can still save a boy, you should. The easiest thing in the world is to kick him off the squad. I don't think an administrator is evaluated by the number of people he can fire. I'd rather think that he is evaluated by the number of people he can get along with. If you go out looking, you're going to find a lot of things you don't like. You have to use common sense; allow for human errors.

"Once a circus came to town. This was on a Friday. We were playing Southern that Saturday. I told the boys, 'I want to see you in bed at ten o'clock. I don't want to see any of you going to that circus. I don't want to see you down there. I'm coming down there to check on you.' So Pete [Pete Griffin, his top assistant] and I walked around, didn't see anybody and headed out of the gate. Somebody yelled, 'Hey, Coach.' I turned around and seated at the very top of the Ferris Wheel was Willie Galimore, my left halfback, and Al Frazier, my right half. I looked at Pete and said, 'Pete, did you hear anything?' He said, 'No, I didn't hear anything, Coach.' I said, 'I didn't either, let's go.' Galimore and Frazier won that game for me the next day. There are just some things you aren't supposed to see.

"I had one coach who got in more trouble. He'd go out of his way to get in trouble. He sneaked around and was always reporting some misconduct on the part of the boys to me. I said, 'Honey, don't go around looking for trouble. You can find enough trouble without looking for it.' "

Gaither's compromising extended to a habit most coaches will not tolerate—smoking. Jake, himself a chain-smoker, only asked that the players not smoke in front of a coach, another student, or the faculty. Yet, he forbade drinking alcoholic beverages under any conditions and once dismissed a player from the team for drinking beer. He says he opposed drinking because he did not want a player insulting a coach.

It took liquor or poor grades to get a player suspended from the squad, for Jake did not cut players. Each year about one hundred players would try out and almost half would quit.

"I didn't cut a half-dozen boys the whole time I was coaching," Jake says. "We would make preseason training so tough that they'd quit themselves. We called it getting the 'white eyes.' The boys who couldn't take it just dropped out and that's when we wanted them to drop out. If they can't take three or four weeks of grind, it's good riddance. They have to pay the price for the Rattlers, even if it's blood. The boy who sticks with it through three or four weeks, he's got something that we want in a football player. He may be a long time coming around, but when he does, you got yourself something."

Those that did survive the grueling practices were a close group. Usually the older players made sure training rules were adhered to through their Honors Court; they would assign players extra wind sprints and exercises for violating the rules. One year a member of the Honors Court beat another FAMU student who was caught having sexual intercourse with a girl on the football field. The zealots charged that the couple had "desecrated" the Rattlers' house and the guy should therefore have the hell beaten out of him. The boy was badly beaten, although to this day it is not known if it was a successful exorcism.

Coaching, even without zealots, is a demanding profession, perhaps more so off-season than during the regular season. Ohio State's Woody Hayes drives a pickup truck so he can catch a quick nap when he's on the road recruiting or making a speech. John McKay, former University of California coach and now coach of the NFL's Tampa Bay Buccaneers, admits, "My worst extremes of emotion are when I'm consistently winning or consistently losing. If I have a winning streak going, the fear of defeat crawls at me and I catch myself thinking I must not lose. A coach will never escape this pressure, no matter how dazzling his record is."

Darrell Royal of Texas amplifies, "You hurt after a loss. You actually physically ache, from your hairline to your toenail, especially if you have blown a championship. Every loss you take is an insult to your talent, your ability."

Alabama's Bear Bryant admits that a few years ago he had to stop on his way to the office every morning—to throw up.

Gaither, perhaps because he has experienced so few defeats, says he didn't undergo the usual vicissitudes of coaching. He says he slept well before and after each game and did not have ulcers or the other stomach disorders that often accompany persistent wear on the nervous system.

While other coaches replay their last loss, Gaither agonizes over what he calls his failures—the players that got sent to jail and those who, like most of his assistant coaches, were married more than once.

"People ask me, 'How's Sadie?' I say, 'Sadie is alright. If

I grunt, she grunts. If I'm alright, she's alright.' She is an ideal wife. You can attribute ninety percent of the success I've had to her. She's level-headed, she's an idealist, she's frugal, and she's an ideal housekeeper. She knew you were coming and she got up at five o'clock and wiped off every picture in this place. So many of my coaches make mistakes in marriage. If the wives don't get along [with their husbands], it shows in the coaches. We tried to get a boy here from Nebraska and he came down. We interviewed him and he wanted to take the job, but his wife had never been South and she was complaining about this and about that. So he said, 'Coach, I can't come—my wife won't let me. If it ain't right in the kitchen, it won't be right on the field.'

"One of my biggest failures is that somehow I haven't advised my boys wisely in marriage, which is a delicate thing to do. Somehow or another, good boys under my influence—good boys on the football field—will make bad marriages. My coaches are the same way. I think every coach I had on my staff except one has been married either two or three times. So many of my boys make bad marriages.

"One night I was talking to the kids about the game and I said, 'I want to talk to you about another thing.' I said, 'I got so many of my boys making bad marriages. Have you ever thought to consider what the wedding vow means?' So I quoted it to them: 'I take this woman to be my lawfully wedded wife. To love, to cherish, to protect until in death do we part.' I said, 'Do you ever think about that? Your wife comes first—before Mama, before Papa, before sister, before brother. That's a hard thing to accept.' I said, 'When I got married, it was hard for me to accept that my wife came before my mother. The wife is the closest thing you have—living or dead. She comes Number One and it doesn't say this should be a temporary situation. It says 'until in death do ye part.' And I talked along those lines. It was the only time I talked to the kids about marriage. That's the one thing that my kids get in trouble more about than anything else. Sometime it's the girl's fault; sometimes it's the boy's fault."

Gaither also feels he failed Steve Scruggs, the last quarterback he coached, who was later convicted of possessing marijuana. Gaither personally recruited the 6-foot-1 southpaw and calls him one of the best, if not the best, quarterbacks he has ever coached.

"Jake just walked into town one day and took Steve back with him," Scruggs's mother says. "Tuskegee had been calling and wiring almost daily. But Coach Gaither seemed to take Steve by surprise and captivated him. They have been awfully nice at Florida A&M."

And Scruggs had been awfully nice to Florida A&M en route to breaking most of the school's passing records. Among the records he still holds are: best passing percentage in one season (59.3); most yards passing in a single game (276) and season (1,576); longest completion (81 yards); and most passes completed in a game (20) and season (129).

Jake's voice is soft and his eyes grow misty when he speaks of Scruggs.

"I fought like hell for him," he says. "I broke down and cried in court the last time they had his trial. I didn't know it [crying] was going to happen; I never dreamed it was going to happen. He was on probation and they were trying to revoke it. I pleaded for the boy. The judge made him serve four weeks in the local jail and let him come out on weekends; he didn't revoke his probation. I broke on the stand. The boy broke. His mother and father were as sweet as can be. The boy could have gone into professional ball and been great. I feel that after being under my supervision for three or four years, he shouldn't get in that kind of trouble. I couldn't see any evidence of it on the football field. He was always in condition and I still don't believe he was on it when I was coaching him. The next year I wasn't coaching. I believe had I been his coach, I would have kept him out of it. He was a junior when I quit coaching in sixty-nine. He was the last quarterback I had. He was the one who beat Tampa and Grambling. Somewhere I failed."

Gaither talked about other players who, in his opinion, had failed in life.

"I got a letter from a guard who is in jail for narcotics," he said dejectedly. "He robbed a bank. He wrote twice and I haven't answered his letters. Of all the boys that I've had, I counted up to six who went bad from high school all the way through college. Two were alcoholics, one was caught stealing, two were involved in dope—and there's one more somewhere. My batting average is poor, and it's poor for the Mamas and Papas, too . . . the teachers and the presidents."

Although he does not agonize over it, Gaither is deeply pained over the death of Oliver Joyce, a freshman who died on the football field just before the 1959 season; it was Gaither's only fatality in twenty-five years, but there have been several at FAMU since his retirement. Joyce, a native of Jacksonville, was participating in a tackling drill when the accident occurred. He was hospitalized through the team's first three games and asked his team-mates to win the fourth one against Bethune-Cookman for him. They did, defeating their opponent 68–6. Joyce died shortly after hearing the score.

"He was a quarterback who was going both ways," Jake says. "He had put his head in there on a shoulder tackle; his knee hit his chin guard, snapped his head back, and broke his neck. It snapped his spinal cord. He was an only son. We raised about ten thousand dollars in five or six years to give to his parents."

Gaither sits up in his chair, and his mood changes as he discusses another unpleasant subject—officiating. His voice grows louder and his words flow faster:

"The biggest letdown for me was when my boys got in trouble or we lost a game because of poor officiating," he says eagerly. "I was tougher on officials if we won a game because of bad officiating. It puts a coach in a helluva spot. You teach a boy the right way to block but some dumb official—a dentist who has been pulling teeth all week and picks up a rule book fifteen minutes before a game and goes on the field—becomes an authority. That makes me mad as hell. Here I am, I've dedicated my life to this work and here's a guy who sells insurance all week, and he suddenly becomes an authority. Then to have some dumb klutz like that mess up your game when you're trying to teach your boys sportsmanship and fair play. What in the devil are you going to tell the boy next week? It's hard to tell that fellow he has to play by the rules and regulations.

You can't go around alibiing. A good sport doesn't go around alibiing as a rule when he loses a game. But what are you going to do when it's obvious the officials have been paid off? After forty-two years of coaching, in high school and college, I have come to the conclusion that the majority of the officials that have worked my games didn't have character. That mistakes weren't mistakes of the head, but mistakes of the heart. I've seen officials who were hometown officials.

"We were playing Alabama A and M and one was the back judge. We threw a pass to a boy named John Eason; he was a tremendous pass receiver and he had great speed —he ran around a nine-eight [9.8 seconds in the 100-yard dash.] And he got behind the defense and into the end zone. The ball hit him in the end zone. Sitting on the bench, I felt he caught the ball in field and took two steps before he got out of bounds. But I wanted to satisfy myself by seeing the film. And the film showed clearly that the boy caught the ball at least three yards in the end zone and took another step before he went out of bounds. This official was as close to him as I am to you," Gaither says, pointing to a reporter sitting six feet away.

"He called no touchdown. I knew he didn't make a mistake of the head, he made a mistake here," Gaither says, thumping his heart. "So I wrote the commissioner and said, 'As long as I'm head coach at Florida A and M, never assign this man to my game. Under no conditions will I accept him.' I had another occasion when we played against Xavier University. A defensive back named Jasper Sanders, who is now a minister in Tampa, batted down a ball at the point of contact and the official called interference. There was a little back judge who hadn't called a foul all night. Nobody knew he was in the ball game. He threw his handkerchief in the air and he jumped two or three feet up in the air, calling interference. I said, 'Now, all that work I spent teaching our boys pass defense and here's a dumb klutz overruling everything that the rules provide for.' He called that foul just to be seen. He hadn't been noticed in the game and he hadn't made any important decisions. I blackballed him.

"When I went to Southern University I knew that I had hell in officials. I told the boys this: 'You got to be at least two touchdowns better than the other team to win. Just expect that kind of officiating.' Rudy [Rudy Hubbard, the present FAMU coach] ran into it two years ago. I said, 'Rudy, you can look for that. They hate Florida's guts—the officials just as much as the players because we've been winning so much. So, don't expect to get a break—be surprised if you do get one.' Now the best officiating I have gotten while I was coaching was in the Central Intercollegiate Athletic Association (CIAA). The poorest officiating, without a doubt, was at Tennessee State and Southern.

"Here's the gimmick they got at Southern. Alright, you fight like hell and hold a team at midfield or hold them on the thirty- or forty-yard line. On third down the quarterback will get the ball and run ten yards behind the line of scrimmage. The end will go down to the one-yard line and the quarterback will throw a long pass to this end, and they'll call interference on the one-yard line. First down and goal. That's the favorite trick in the Southwestern Athletic Conference.

"We played a SWAC team in the Classic one year, and the team that plays in the Classic has the right to bring half of the game's officials from their conference. So they brought one of the officials who had done that to us at Southern. We were winning the game and they pulled that trick on us. As the half ended, I walked out on the field and said, 'Now, this trick that you folks have been pulling off in the SWAC, I'm aware of it.' I said, 'All the people in Florida know that you do it. You called one just a while ago. If you call another one, I won't guarantee your safety. These people in Florida are serious about their football, and they're liable to tear you to pieces before you can get out to the gate.' I said, 'If I were you, I'd be very careful in calling those deep passes interference unless you're absolutely sure and everybody can see that you're making a good call. These blacks in Florida will tear you to pieces—piece by piece. I'm not going to make an effort to protect you. I'm going to let them have you.' I didn't have any more trouble. That's all I could say. I wanted to put the fear of God in his heart because he could have killed us. You take a guy who's smart and he is a good official, he can cut your throat right and left and you'd never know it. We ran into it time and time again.

"If we could have ghost officials—you couldn't see them, all you could do was hear the whistle—we'd get good officiating. But some have got to be seen, despite the fact that you tell them that people don't spend their money to see those striped shirts walking up and down the field—they spend their money to see those boys play. I tell them, 'If you guys could disassociate yourselves from your own self-importance, we'd get decently called games.' But their flair for attention and desire to be seen got in the way. I would worry about what kind of officiating we were going to get sometimes more than how our boys were going to play."

If anything or anyone raised Gaither's ire more than officiating, it is John Merritt, the eminently successful football coach at Tennessee State University in Nashville. Merritt, who completed his fourteenth season in the fall of 1976, has a career record of 173 wins, 54 losses, and 8 ties. His record at Tennessee State is even more impressive: 113–22–4.

But the friction between Merritt and Gaither is deeper than the two of them vying for success; the competition between the schools—among the bands, in displaying fashion, and everything else—is more bitter than Texas versus Arkansas or Ohio State versus Michigan. The game was an event in which the all-male bands competed as fiercely as the football players, and like the football squads, they scouted each other. Both of them have performed on national television during halftime at professional games, and both bands feature fast-paced marching, flamboyant body and instrument movements and exceptionally good music. The FAMU band has been timed in at an incredible 329 steps per minute—as opposed to the regular 24 to 80 steps a minute—and Tennessee State's band marches at roughly the same speed, depending on which team is ahead at halftime.

"The high point of the FAMU game was to see which band was the best," says Mrs. Elaine Harris Spearman, a Tennessee State alumnus. "I was going with a guy in the band then and they'd practice night and day for weeks before the game. We *had* to come off better, and we usually did. Some students who didn't like football came at halftime just to see the bands.

"FAMU was our archrival; you just had to go. Grambling and homecoming were exciting, too, but not like FAMU. The students at Tennessee State were cleaner than the teachers, anyway—they were sky clean. Students fell out in droves for the FAMU game. It was the fashion show of all fashion shows. People came from all over for that game, and the hotels were booked months in advance."

Michael T. Key, another Tennessee State graduate and now a city official in East St. Louis, Illinois, viewed the game from a purely athletic standpoint. His words are crisp and resonant.

"There was only one game at Tennessee State," he says. "And that was against FAMU. We could be nine-and-one for the year, but if we lost to FAMU, we considered it a disastrous season."

Tennessee State was the only school on FAMU's regular schedule and Merritt the only opposing coach with a better record than Gaither and his teams.* Coincidentally, the series began in 1945, Jake's first season as head coach, and, going into the 1977 season, Tennessee State leads the series, 14 wins to 5 wins for Florida A&M. From 1945 to 1965—a period in which the teams opposed each other six times—each team alternated in winning the contest. FAMU won in 1945 at Tallahassee, 20–18. In 1956,

---

*The only other coach to come close to beating Gaither in three games or more is Eddie Robinson of Grambling. They have split four games.

Tennessee State won in Nashville, 41–39. The 1962 game was won by FAMU in Tallahassee, 20–0. The next year Tennessee State won, 14–12, at home. In 1964 FAMU won at home, 22–20. Then in 1965, TSU began a three-game winning streak: 45–6, 29–0, and 32–8, thanks to exceptional quarterback Eldridge Dickey, nicknamed "The Lord's Prayer."

Dickey is generally considered the best black quarterback to play the college game and many feel he would have done better in the pros than either Jim Harris of the Rams or "Jefferson Street" Joe Gilliam, formerly of the Pittsburgh Steelers. Unfortunately, no one will ever know, because the Oakland Raiders used him as a flanker. In four years at Tennessee State—from 1964 through 1967—Dickey led his team to a 34–5–1 record. He passed for 6,641 yards and 74 touchdowns. He was a four-time *Pittsburgh Courier* All-America choice.

Before the 1968 game, the year Joe Gilliam followed Dickey at TSU, Gaither gave one of his emotion-charged pregame pep talks. "Boys, I don't ask you for much," he moaned. "It's not my nature to ask my team to do something for me, but I want this game. I want it more than any game the Rattlers have played during my coaching career and I'm asking you to win one for me." The team was so charged-up that it hit the Tennessee State ball carrier so hard on the opening kickoff that he fumbled. FAMU recovered and went on to win 32–13.

Over the years, however, TSU has specialized in spoiling otherwise perfect seasons for Gaither. For example, in 1956—the year that Willie Galimore set more than a half-dozen school records—both teams were undefeated and were playing for the mythical National Black Championship; Tennessee State won 41–39, despite a 4-touchdown performance by Galimore. In 1962 and 1964, FAMU lost just one game—to TSU. And in Gaither's last year, 1969, FAMU had a perfect record except for a 33–20 loss to Tennessee State.

Jake Gaither speaks disparagingly of the Tennessee State coach and thinks less of Merritt than he does of any other coach or person he has known. Merritt's dislike for Gaither, at least when they opposed each other, was also strong.

"Here's one thing he did," Jake says eagerly. "We were playing him up there. It was halftime and we finally got off the field to go to the dressing room. It takes about ten minutes to get off the field, and you don't have but fifteen minutes between halves. His dressing room was adjoining ours. He just burst the door open and came in. He said, 'Jake, your sons of bitches are playing dirty football.' That's what he said. He stood right in the door. I said, 'Merritt, if you don't get out of that door, I'm going to turn this football team loose on you and they'll tear you to pieces.' Well, he laughed about it. What he wanted to do was upset me at halftime when I was trying to correct mistakes. That's about the worst thing I've ever experienced in my life.

"Another time we were playing a game and we could never get beyond the thirty-five–yard line. Every time we'd start a drive, we'd come up with a fifteen-yard penalty. They used officials from the Midwest Conference, which went defunct because it didn't have enough teams. But they had some defunct Midwest Conference officials.

The only teams in the conference were Kentucky State and Tennessee State. If they [the officials] worked at all, they had to work for either Kentucky State or Tennessee State. They belonged to no conference and, like the players, they would do anything. In this game when we couldn't get past the thirty-five, they threw a pass and we got an interception. And our boy was running for a touchdown right up the sidelines by the the Tennessee State bench. A boy got off the bench and ran out on the field and tackled him. The officials ruled a touchdown. Merritt put that boy in the game and he played from then on out. Had it been one of my boys that did a thing like that, I'd have sent him to the dressing room. I would have gotten him off the bench and disqualified him forever from playing football.

"Now the last straw on the camel's back was when we went up there in nineteen sixty-nine. We were having our pregame warmups. In walking around the field, I saw a telephone hookup to the pressbox on his side. So I went to Merritt and I said, 'We don't have a telephone.' He said, 'Yes, I know.' I said, 'If you have one for yourself, you're certainly obligated to furnish one for your opponent.' He said, 'You should bring your own telephone or walkie-talkie. Hell, we don't furnish them.' I said, 'Well, switch sides with me—you go on my side and I'll come over on yours. Then I'll have the same advantage that you have.' He said, 'Oh, no.' I said, 'Well, there won't be any game. I have my bus. I got transportation back to Florida and I don't have a damn thing to do with your gate receipts. Suppose you explain to the crowd why I'm not playing.' The boys were on the field—they had won the toss. I said,

'Go on back to the bench, there won't be a game.' "

Gaither says Merritt acquiesced, but later used the telephones anyway. When told of the charges, Merritt replies, "We have only one set of phones. The visiting team usually brings its own here and we wouldn't play unless we used ours. I didn't like the way he approached the subject." In response to the charge of poor officiating, Merritt asks, "He complains after what he gives me down there?"

Jake did not soften his criticism.

"The cards were so stacked that Notre Dame, Georgia, and Florida all together couldn't have won," he said, referring to the 1969 loss. "I'm not a coach who alibis for losing, but the spirit of football is one where one team does not have an unfair advantage over the other. There was an advantage in Nashville." Gaither told the press that he would never play Tennessee State in Nashville again.*

Merritt, who is still head coach at Tennessee State, says he respects Gaither and credits him with improving the status of football at black colleges. He seems genuinely shocked that Jake dislikes him as a person, but refuses to criticize him. Rather, he speaks highly of him and the trail he has pioneered.

"If Jake had made it public that he was going to bow out that year, I may have let him win that last one," he says. "I revere him just that much. He's a competitor and I

---

*This was an empty threat, because Jake had already told FAMU president Benjamin L. Perry, Jr., that he was retiring after the 1969 football season. In his official letter of resignation, dated December 17, 1969, Gaither wrote, "As I indicated to you last spring, I want to be relieved of Head Football Coaching duties at the close of the 1969 football season and retain the duties of Athletic Director and Professor of Physical Education. . . ."

knew he wanted to beat me as much as I wanted to beat him. But it was purely psychological warfare with me. You had to try to get him upset because he had a tremendous knack for getting his kids up for a ball game. But I think his kids got to a point where even they didn't believe they could beat us.

"It was a great series. I'll tell you this: When Jake retired it lost a lot of its personal appeal for me. It was no challenge anymore. Even though we lost in 1975, it's not a challenge anymore.*

"The whole preparation for beating Jake was psychological. I think that most people were beaten when they put Jake on their schedule. I think Jake's name—as well as his teams—was such a household word. His record was so phenomenal that people just didn't believe they could beat him. They would go into the ball game, I think, not believing they could beat him.

"I would always work myself up and get ready for Jake. I would always do a special job, not only on the boys, but on myself. I would always try to find something that would get him upset mentally." He, too, mentions his entering Jake's dressing room at halftime as an example of one of his ploys. Merritt said also that the competition of nerves got so fierce that Gaither and his assistants refused to attend the social function that he usually held for Gaither the night before their game.**

*Florida A&M defeated Tennessee State, 20–0, in 1975, the first year FAMU has ever beat TSU at home, and ending a TSU six-game winning streak.
**As a matter of custom, the host black coach usually gives a party for the visiting coach and his assistants in his home. No one knows when this trend started, but it has generally been observed throughout the years.

Merritt denies he allowed the player who came off the bench to save a touchdown to remain in the game. "Jake's wrong about that," he says. "I didn't play him. Sam played in one, maybe two, games his whole college career.

"Sam Smith, who is a high school coach at North High School here in Nashville, is from Jackson, Mississippi, and a running back," Merritt says, recalling the incident. "We kid Sam all the time that that was the most famous thing he did while he was at Tennessee State," he says, laughing.

In a more serious vein, Merritt says, "I have been accused of pushing Sam on the field, telling him to 'Hit him,' but I was nowhere near him when that happened. The boy broke loose on an interception—he intercepted near their own goal line. As he came up the sidelines it was quite evident that he was going all the way. I believe it was Major Hazelton. Major was on that crack quarter-mile team,* he was tremendously fast and when he came by our bench, old Sam just stepped out there about a yard or two and put the shoulder under him just as beautiful. Of course, they awarded him a touchdown."

He adds, "Jake is the only black coach that ever made the American Football Coaches Association 'Coach of the Year.' That is one of the few honors I've never had and I'll probably never get it. But Jake's had that. Unless Eddie [Robinson] can get it while he's president, no other black coach will ever get it; you don't have enough blacks to put you in. Jake had rapport with guys who could control the

---

*The FAMU relay team of Bob Hayes (9.1), Alfred Austin (9.8), Robert Paremore (9.4), and Robert Harris (9.4) became the first team to win the Drake Relays three consecutive years.

votes. You take guys like Bear Bryant; all fourteen of his assistants probably voted for Jake. This has to be a tremendous honor; none of us has been able to get it. I finished the nineteen seventy-three season Number One in both polls—AP and UPI—and we were undefeated. We had the Number One draft choice [Ed "Too Tall" Jones] and I didn't get it. If I didn't get it then, I won't get it.

"Had it not been for Jake, I don't think Eddie Robinson would be president of the American Football Coaches Association, as he is today. I think it was through the efforts of Jake that this became available to him. And regardless of how you feel—and I used to hate him with a passion, but I had utmost respect for him—he certainly has served and you can't get around that."

Although Merritt is respectful of Jake's accomplishments, even appreciative of them, the kindest thing Gaither says about Merritt in a thirty-minute tirade is, "Merritt doesn't have to do the things he does. He has good personnel. He could be a straight, honest coach and probably have just as good a record as he's got now. He's the only coach I can say that about. I wouldn't go across the street to speak to Merritt."

9

The Big One

November 29, 1969, was a momentous day for college football. Appropriately enough, it was in college football's centennial year that Florida A&M, a predominantly black university, was to play the predominantly white University of Tampa in the South's first interracial football game. But this game would have been exciting even if both teams had been polka dot. Tampa, which was ranked Number Six among small colleges in America, had won eight consecutive games since losing its season opener to the University of Akron. Florida A&M, rated sixteenth, had won six of its seven games, the only loss being to archrival Tennessee State.

The fact that the game was being played at all was a testament to the enduring nature of the much-maligned black college football, which had its origin on Thanksgiving Day in 1892, just twenty-three years after Rutgers defeated Princeton in the country's first intercollegiate football game. Although much has been written about that first game, very little has been published about the first game between Livingstone College and Biddle University, two black colleges.

For the record, Biddle, now known as Johnson C. Smith

University, traveled across state from Charlotte to play Livingstone College in Salisbury, North Carolina. The game, which was divided into two 45-minute halves, was played in a snowstorm and subfreezing temperatures. Biddle scored the first touchdown—which then counted for 5 points—and was about to score a second when J. W. Walker, the Livingstone captain, tackled a Biddle player, causing a fumble. William J. Trent, Sr., who later became president of Livingstone, scooped up the errant ball and ran it into the end zone for what he thought was the tying touchdown. However, Trent's run was nullified when the lone official (a white law student at the University of North Carolina) upheld Biddle's contention that their ball carrier had been tackled out of bounds on the snow-covered field thus making the ball dead at that point. The game ended in a 5–0 victory for the visiting Biddle squad. The Livingstone yearbook noted forty years later:

> In 1892 several young men . . . decided to inaugurate football at Livingstone. To that end, an order was placed for one of the regulation footballs from Spalding's [sic] . . . each man chipping in and paying for it. Then the fellows began to work putting cleats on their everyday shoes until after practice, when they would be taken off. Old clothes were patched and padded up and these constituted the togs of the first Livingstone team.

Trent, whose son William, Jr., was to become assistant director of personnel for Time, Inc., later recalled that the team's football uniforms were made by the women in the school's Industrial Arts Department. He also noted proudly that his was probably the best of the group because he was dating the director of the sewing department at the time. Within the next few years, other black colleges—Lincoln University in Pennsylvania, Howard, Tuskegee, Atlanta, and Shaw—established football teams. During that period, blacks—particularly William H. Lewis, an All-America center at Harvard—were gaining national recognition while playing for predominantly white universities.

For blacks throughout Florida and across the nation, the game between Florida A&M and the University of Tampa would provide a glorious opportunity to still critics who had charged, since the day Biddle first defeated Livingstone College, that football at black colleges was inferior to that played by their white counterparts.

The game was Gaither's chance to prove two points: first, that black colleges could compete against white institutions, and even emerge victorious; second, that an interracial game could be staged peacefully in the Deep South.

The 46,477 fans began filling Tampa Stadium early to witness history in the making and their favorite team win, not necessarily in that order. Ultimately, the FAMU fans were not disappointed, although at times it appeared that the favored Tampa Spartans would march over the Rattlers, leaving their fangs lying harmless on the football field.

In the dressing room, Gaither, who was about to coach the penultimate game of his forty-second–year career, worked tirelessly to get his Rattlers coiled for the game and Leon McQuay, Tampa's star running back.

"I want you to go out there and stretch that Leon McQuay," Gaither exhorted.

"Hubba, Hubba!" the team replied loudly.

"I want you to tackle him high," Gaither urged.

"Hubba, Hubba!" shouted the Rattlers.

"I want you to tackle him low," Gaither said fervidly.

"Hubba, Hubba!" came the response.

"I want you to tackle him in the belly."

"Hubba, Hubba!"

"Then I want you to s-t-r-e-t-c-h him!"

"Hubba, Hubba!" chanted the Rattlers.

After prayer and announcement of the starting lineups, the team rushed on field for its calisthenics and the coin toss. Tampa won the toss and elected to receive the kickoff; FAMU chose to defend the north goal. From the opening moments, the game was action-filled. FAMU's kickoff went out of bounds and Horace Lovett had to kick off again, this time from 5 yards farther back. The second kick was returned to the Tampa 20-yard line. Four plays later, Tampa was on FAMU's 6-yard line, but the Rattlers held and took over after Tampa missed a field goal try.

Beginning on their own 20, A&M scored seven plays later, on a 19-yard pass from Steve Scruggs to Alfred Sykes. The point after was good, making the score 7–0 in FAMU's favor. Tampa scored 6 minutes later on a run by Leon McQuay around left end. The conversion was successful, tying the score at 7–7. Midway in the second quarter, FAMU scored again on a 15-yard run by quarterback Steve Scruggs over right tackle; the extra point gave FAMU a 14–7 lead. Tampa came back within three minutes to tie the score 14–14, which stood at halftime.

Florida A&M threatened to pull away by scoring two touchdowns in the third quarter to take a commanding, at least for then, 28–14 lead. But McQuay put the Spartans back in the game, scoring a touchdown with fifty-seven seconds left in the third quarter.

In the final quarter Tampa scored early on a 36-yard pass from QB Jim DelGaizo to Paul Orndorf, and tied the score 28–28 with less than 12 minutes remaining in the game.

Florida A&M got a break in the next series of downs when pass interference was called on Tampa as Scruggs attempted to pass to Kent Schoolfield on third-and-six. FAMU converted two key third-down situations and on third and goal at the Tampa 4-yard line, halfback Hubert Ginn scampered around left end for 4 yards and tumbled into the end zone with 4:55 left in the game. The point after was missed, making the score Florida A&M 34; Tampa 28. After a key interception by FAMU's Harry Passmore and an unsuccessful FAMU field goal from 20 yards out, Tampa quickly drove from its own 20-yard line to the FAMU 14. Then the Spartans failed on four straight pass attempts and FAMU took over on downs. Quarterback Steve Scruggs ran two plays and the game was over. Final score: Florida A&M 34, Tampa 28.

Gaither stayed up all night savoring the fruits of his team's victory.

"The game vindicated my belief that a game of this type could be carried off in an atmosphere of peaceful tranquility and good sportsmanship," he says. "It also helped destroy the myth that black football teams are not on a par with white colleges in the small college division." Gaither says he was proud that the game was played in Florida, noting, "You can't go any farther south than

Florida. I don't know where you'd go unless you went out in the Gulf. Now, if that happens in the deepest part of the South, I think it will be a new beginning."

A twinkle still appears in Jake's eyes at the mention of the game.

"The Tampa game was a great game," he says, exuberantly. "It was just like it had been written out of a story book. The author always tries to make his stories have a happy ending where everyone loves each other and lives happily ever after. Well, if we had written the script for the Tampa game, we couldn't have come up with a better ending. In the first place, it was an interracial game— that's what it amounted to, although we tried to soft-pedal it because I wanted to prove to the people of Florida and the Southland that a game of this type could go on without any unusual or bad results.

"So we approached the game just as another football game, between two good teams, both of whom wanted to win. We were making no special effort to prepare our boys for this game any moreso than we would in preparing for any tough game. It was just incidental that our opponents happened to be white. Well, that was the angle that I kept before our boys and the press."

Gaither is appreciative of the efforts of Fran Curci, the Tampa coach. "Fran Curci is a fine fellow, a fine sport, and he used the same technique in dealing with his boys and the press. I believe he got his boys to believe that; I believe the two of us got the public to feel the same way. We had forty-seven thousand people at that game, about equally divided between black and white, and it seemed to me that both groups wanted this type of game to go on without any friction. They just wanted a hard, tough, clean football game with good sportsmanship displayed by players and good sportsmanship displayed by the fans.

"That's the reason I say it was just like out of a story book, because that's just the way it happened. From the opening whistle until the game was over, there was action. It started out with action. You saw some of the best passes that you'll ever want to see. You saw some of the best punting. It was just a good game from beginning to end. The score was seven-zero, seven-seven, fourteen-seven, twenty-eight–fourteen, twenty-eight–twenty-eight and ended up thirty-four–twenty-eight. Now, you couldn't ask for a more evenly fought contest than that—good clean football.

"I don't want to underestimate the contribution that Fran Curci made to that situation. He was such a good sport—his reaction after the game was so genuine and so honest that the followers of Fran Curci had to take his lead. When the game was over he came across the field running as though he was taking off on a hundred-yard dash; he was not strutting. He ran up to me and said, 'Jake, you deserve to win.' Well, nobody had left the stadium then. He helped control that situation. That man did a great thing—he didn't have to do it. I think all the way through Curci had a leveling influence upon militant groups; I probably wielded it on my side. We came up with the fulfillment of a dream: It can happen. I don't think there can be any question in anybody's mind about that.

"I went to the professional game the next day—the Patriots against the Dolphins. Honest to goodness, we almost went to sleep. The professional game was so dull and uninteresting that the people around me complained. The play looked slow, the backs looked slow, the punting was bad, the passing was bad, and they just played a bad game. I think it was all because we had seen such fireworks the night before."

When the final smoke had settled, the statistics were about even:

	Tampa	*FAMU*
First Downs	23	22
Yards Rushing	138	321
Yards Passing	423	189
Passes Attempted	47	22
Passes Completed	23	14
Interceptions By	1	3
Fumbles Lost	0	1
Punts	3 (47.3 yd. avg.)	2 (48 yd. avg.)
Yards Penalized	47	80

Score by Quarter:

Tampa	7	7	7	7	–	28
FAMU	7	7	14	6	–	34

In the years since his retirement, Gaither has admitted that far from viewing the Tampa game as just another contest, he wanted to win it more than any he has been involved in.

"We wanted the Tampa game regardless of how I played it down," he now concedes. "I knew deep down in my heart what the winning of that game would mean. We [the coaches] wanted it, the boys wanted it. But I did want to make it clear to them that the whole world didn't depend on it."

A few years earlier Gaither had become distressed over

what he perceived as a loss of discipline among his players. While other coaches throughout the country were
complaining publicly of what they thought was a "new
athlete," the type unwilling to accept traditions blindly,
Jake never envisioned that the same thing could happen
at Florida A&M. Yet, the problem did strike home.

Gaither was awakened late one night by a telephone
call from one of the dorm directors, who said some football players were creating a disturbance in the residence
hall. A groggy Jake Gaither dressed and drove his Lincoln
Continental to the campus. He met a few players outside
and inquired about the disruption. He was told the problem began when some upperclassmen decided to shave
the freshmen's heads. When told the room number of the
"barber shop," Jake went upstairs; he was stunned when
he saw that the barber and leader of the disturbance was,
of all people, the captain of the team. Gaither stopped at
the door and asked rhetorically, "What have I got here?"
before turning and walking out.

Jake met with his assistants the next day, apologized for
letting discipline slip out of his control, and announced
that from that time forward, he would no longer rely on
the senior players for leadership as he had in the past.
Instead, the players would be lectured about morals,
school spirit, good manners, and discipline. Jake was still
working on the problem as he was ending his final season
as coach. In his mind, he was not certain that he would
ever be able to bring back those Boy Scout virtues that
had been cherished throughout his reign. That is, he
didn't know until after the Tampa game. As his team
prepared to return to Tallahassee, Jake was heartened.

After he boarded the bus before its return trip home—he would not travel with the team because he had a speaking engagement—he announced that the team could have Monday off before its final game. Just as Jake finished his statement, Carlmon Jones, a senior tackle, said the team did not want to have the day off, preferring to practice for its last game. Jake asked if the other players were in agreement; they responded in the affirmative. Gaither instructed his assistants to hold practice.

Until then, Gaither had told only President Perry that he planned to quit after the 1969 season, although his assistants had expected as much. He called a meeting of his assistants after the bus incident and said, "Listen, kids. Now we got back what we lost—that's discipline. I won't be with you after next week—that's my last game. For God's sake, don't you lose it. Don't ever let this get away from the squad again. We got back what we lost."

After the victory over the University of Tampa and seeing the return of discipline to the Rattler squad, Jake Gaither had just one game remaining to coach, against Grambling State University in the Orange Blossom Classic. Grambling has a rich athletic tradition, although its sports information director, Collie J. Nicholson, jokes that the school is so far in the Louisiana woods that in order to reach the campus, one must travel by airplane, then by bus, and the remaining miles via covered wagon.

It has been argued that Grambling turns out so many exceptional players because there is little else to do in the town, which is barely larger than a service station. Some students protested what they called an overemphasis on athletics in the late 1960s, saying "the school yearbook looks like *Sports Illustrated."* Although school officials may take issue with that opinion, there is little disagreement that its athletic program has been successful and that the school is better known throughout the world because of it.

The FAMU-Grambling game marked an end to an era of sorts; it marked the last time the Orange Blossom Classic would be limited to black colleges. Further, it ended an era in which FAMU often looked to the powerful Southwest Athletic Conference, which is generally considered the most potent of the black conferences, for an opponent in the Classic.

Jake had made the decision to desegregate the Classic in 1968 after Texas Southern University, then the SWAC champion, had arranged to play Morgan State College, winner of the Central Intercollegiate Athletic Conference crown, on the same day FAMU was playing Alcorn in the Classic. Before the Grambling game, Gaither, referring to his selection of Orange Blossom Classic opponents, told *Miami Herald* Sports Editor Edwin Pope, "We could have filled up the Orange Bowl by playing the University of Tampa. But I stuck to the principle of having only Negro schools. Then the Central Intercollegiate Athletic Association on the East Coast got together with the South West Athletic Conference and decided their champions would play the same date in the Astrodome. It not only hurts our national publicity, but it cuts down on the caliber of possible rivals. That's the thanks we get. We begged them to put their Morgan State–Texas Southern game some other date, but they went ahead anyway. As far as I'm concerned, as long as our president, Dr. B. L. Perry,

Jr., gives me the authority, from now on we will pick the best opponent available—black, white, yellow, purple, or blue."

The game in the Astrodome turned out to be a colossal failure; the few fans who showed up could have been seated comfortably in a telephone booth with plenty of room left to accommodate a repairman. The following year, Gaither invited Jacksonville State, a predominantly white college from Alabama, to play in the Classic. Since that time neither Texas Southern nor Morgan State has played in the OBC, and neither probably will as long as Gaither, who still sits on the school's athletic committee, has anything to say about it.

It is ironic that the game that caused Gaither to open up the Classic to predominantly white teams involved Morgan State. Five years earlier, Gaither had turned to the same Maryland school when SWAC officials voted not to play in the Orange Blossom Classic unless FAMU guaranteed them 37½ percent of the gross instead of an offer of $18,000. Gaither, whose school derives 40 percent of its athletic budget from the game, contended that if he had been forced to give the opposing team 37½ percent, FAMU would have lost $15,000 on the game.

Ultimately, FAMU decided to play Morgan State. After a touchdown by Leroy Kelly put Morgan ahead, 7–0, FAMU rebounded to win, 30–7. The following year FAMU played Grambling, getting its way on the contract and on the field, winning 42–15.

On the night of December 9, 1969, in Miami, Gaither was to deliver his last pep talk. The players converged around the Papa Rattler, and as Gaither began to talk, it was so quiet that one could hear an ant tiptoe on cotton. This speech was not unlike others given earlier in his career, but as Jake paused for effect, accented different words, and flailed his arms, it sounded like a different script.

"This is the last game of the season," he said. "This is the last time that some of you will see each other on the football field. We've got some seniors on our squad who have been with us four years—they're moving out. I'd like for this to be their greatest game."

"Hubba, Hubba!"

"I'd like to feel that this game tonight is a culmination of *everything* that we've been trying to do well this year. Our blocking ought to be the best, our running ought to be the best, our passing and receiving ought to be the best, our tackling ought to be the best. We were going to improve from week to week—this is the last chance to show your improvement. [Pause] We'd very much like to win this ball game. I know you put out heavily last week, but you've got to reach back in that hip pocket and give me all you've got tonight."

"Hubba, Hubba!"

"I want you to realize that this is a tough team—they've got everything to win out there and nothing to lose. If they can knock off the team that made history last week, they want to do it. The fact that they've lost a couple of games doesn't mean a thing in the world. Folks are expecting great things out of you. Let's play the type of ball game that we can play. Keep your poise—don't jump offsides and commit fouls that you shouldn't commit. I want those backs putting both hands on that ball. The ball game today on television—you saw it, too—Texas stayed in the hole because of that fumble and so many mistakes made turning over the ball. They made a tough game out of it. They had to come from the rear to win. But they did it and never let up. The ball game isn't won until the last whistle is blown.

"Now, I haven't been satisfied with your protection of our place kicker for extra points and field goals. He's had two or three of 'em blocked this year. Men have been coming down that middle and blocking some of them. A field goal or extra point can mean the difference between winning and losing. Every time you set there, we want you to swear by all God that nobody's going to block that kick. Give our passer protection, don't let a soul lay a hand on him. Scruggs will deliver. We've got receivers who will catch. They're going to be trying to get us. I want you to get to their passer and lay the wood on him. Start now with the kickoff team."

An assistant called out the names for the kickoff team, "Black, Goodrum, Williams, Lyons, Finnie . . ."

Gaither continued, "I want that kickoff team, if we kick off, to get down; don't let them bring that ball past the twenty. If you can get a fumble down there, we'll move in for a score. I want you to get out fast like you've been doing all year. Don't let them run. They've got a terrific kickoff return man. Locate that ball and close in cautiously. Widen your base, move in on him. I want you to put them in a cup—don't let them get out of there. Receiving team."

Another assistant called out the names of the receivers, "Miller, MacCallister, Barnett, Goodwin . . ."

Gaither directed, "If they kick off to us, I'd like to see you take it all the way. Good blocking, no clipping now. Let's see if we can get these long runs without clipping tonight. Defensive team."

The assistant coach for the defense spoke up, "One of the gutsiest football players I've ever coached won't be here tonight—Wilcox. Starting up front will be Jackson, Amos, Boyd, Times, Stockton, Rogers . . ."

Gaither outlined starting-position preferences. "Our first choice is to receive. Our second choice is to defend that goal with the wind at our back, going this way. Are there any questions? Offensive team."

The assistant coach for the offense called out players' names for positions: "The backfield . . . Scruggs at quarterback, Ginn at halfback, Owens at fullback, Schoolfield at flanker."

With the lineups announced, Gaither concluded with a prayer. "Alright in here. God of the Rattlers, our *good* God, giver of every good and perfect gift. You've been good to us, much better than we deserve. May we always be grateful to Thee. We don't ask for victory, dear God. We ask for a chance for our boys to do their best. These blessings we ask in the name of Jesus, Our Redeemer. Amen."

The team chorused with two bars of "Hubba, Hubba," and went out to defeat Grambling 23–19, allowing Jake to end his coaching career just as he had begun twenty-five years earlier—with a victory.

10

Jake Versus the NFL

Jake Gaither is an institution in Florida. He is venerated by both blacks and whites alike because of his outstanding coaching record, his sagaciousness, his charisma, his moderate views on racial issues, and the many, many contributions he has made to the youth of the state. While other coaches in Florida were being hanged in effigy, Gaither's picture was being hanged in living rooms across the state. At Florida A&M, students, faculty, and alumni have always united to demonstrate their unwavering support for Gaither—win or tie.

The closest Gaither came to having his armor tarnished was in 1971 when, as FAMU's athletic director, he engaged in a protracted controversy with the National Football League.

Briefly, this is what happened: The Miami Dolphins with a 9–2–1 record, the best in the NFL and a half-game lead over the second-place Baltimore Colts, were scheduled to play the defending Super Bowl champion Colts in Miami on Saturday, December 11. The game, next to the last of the season, was crucial to both teams' efforts to enter the playoffs. Three weeks earlier, Miami had won a game between them, 17–14, on a late field goal. The rematch was scheduled to be played at 4:00 P.M. in Miami's Orange Bowl to accommodate the National Broadcasting Company (NBC), but there was one problem—Florida A&M held the contract on the stadium for its Orange Blossom Classic, which was scheduled to be played at 8:00 P.M.

After failing to placate Gaither, NFL Commissioner Alvin "Pete" Rozelle ordered that the game be played in Baltimore so the league could benefit from the broadcast rights. The nationally televised game could not be shown to fans back in the Miami area because of a federal law prohibiting telecast of pro football within a seventy-five– mile radius on the same day a college game is played in the area. Predictably, the Miami fans, already disappointed at not being able to see the game at home, were furious when they learned that they wouldn't be able to view the game on television either.

Let's begin at the beginning.

To fully understand the fans' furor, one must remember that the 1971 season had stirred excitement among rabid Dolphins fans. Quarterback Bob Griese was at that time the NFL's top-rated passer, having completed 115 of 212 passes for 1,816 yards and only 7 interceptions. Wide receiver Paul Warfield had caught a league-leading 11 touchdown passes and his 36 receptions were for 907 yards, giving him a 25.5 average, also the best in the NFL. Running back Larry Csonka had amassed 939 yards and 6 touchdowns in 170 carries, making him the second leading rusher in the conference [John Brockington of the Green Bay Packers was in the lead with 969 yards]. Mercury Morris, a running back, had been a spectacular kickoff returner, averaging 33.5 yards per return in 11 attempts. Placekicker Garo Yepremian was the NFL's leading scorer, having converted 30 of 30 points after touchdowns, and 25 of 35 field goals. Unfortunately, there are no statistics for offensive linemen, but Larry Little was one of, if not the, best guards in professional football.

More than an important football game, the contest also took on added significance to Colts fans, who felt betrayed when Don Shula was spirited away from Baltimore by Dolphin owner Joe Robbie in 1970. Shula's departure was taken especially hard by Colt owner Carroll Rosenbloom, who later became owner of the Los Angeles Rams. Eventually, Rozelle ruled that the Dolphins had tampered with Shula, who was under contract with the Colts at the time, and awarded the Colts Miami's first draft choice in 1971.*
Rosenbloom was fined for saying, "Shula has very few fans among the players and I am not one, either." He also said, "I want a coach who wants to win and my feeling about a head coach is that he be one who must have rapport with his players, that he be fair at all times and, unfortunately, we have not had this since Weeb Eubank left. I decided that Shula could do the job, and we brought him in and he has done a fine job, with the exception of winning the big ones. As you know, he left me with a legacy. I will always be remembered as the first NFL owner to lose the Super Bowl game . . ."

Rosenbloom is still bitter about the incident, and when he was fined in 1975 for criticizing the officiating in one

---

*Tampering is generally defined by the NFL as approaching another club's coach without obtaining the owner's permission.

game, he took the opportunity again to bring up the Shula situation. In a statement, he said, sarcastically, "Since an agreement exists between the owners and NFL Commissioner Pete Rozelle that fines will not be discussed publicly, I am not in a position to elaborate. I helped make the rules and I try to abide by them.

"In 1971, I was notified by Rozelle on a fine in the Don Shula matter. Abiding by league rules, I refused to discuss the matter publicly.

"However, Rozelle saw fit to discuss the fine at the next Super Bowl game when he had a maximum media audience.

"Therefore, I refer you to Rozelle for any further information. I feel certain, if he does not care to elaborate further at this time he will, in all probability, be happy to do so at the upcoming Super Bowl."

But Rosenbloom's dislike for Shula did not approach the anger felt by Dolphin fans, who felt cheated on two counts. The NFL attempted to direct the fans' ire at Gaither, saying that Jake refused to change his starting time to accommodate the game being held in Miami or to waive the blackout.

Bob Cochran, who coordinates TV contracts for the NFL, told reporters that Gaither could allow the telecast. NBC's Miami affiliate, which carried the Dolphins' away game, told Jake that their interpretation of Public Law 87–331 permitted him to waive the blackout. The Miami *Herald* even got a reporter in its Washington bureau to corner an attorney with the Justice Department's antitrust division. The official said that if Jake agreed, the department would not pursue the matter in court.

Yet Gaither held out, saying that this game was unlike the others.

"Those were the one o'clock games," he protested, referring to the times he had allowed past telecasts. "This is a four o'clock game and that will hurt my crowd. The move makes a difference. The pro game will last three hours, and I'm afraid nobody's going to watch it and then come downtown for the Classic. Right now, I'll let them worry about it. I'd say Florida A and M is entitled to some kind of compensation. I've been going along with the pros and television for years. When it came time for them to reciprocate with something positive for us they didn't."

Jake had originally said he was willing to switch his game from 8:00 P.M. to 11:00 A.M., with the proviso that the NFL pay FAMU $100,000. He later reduced that figure to $75,000. It was impractical to change his game to another day, because the University of Miami had a game scheduled the preceding Saturday, and a delay of another week would have been too long because FAMU had already completed its regular season. Gaither also feared that holding the game on a Friday night would hurt his gate, which depends to a large degree on alumni traveling from all parts of the state.

The NFL sent Buddy Young, the ex-Illinois and Baltimore Colts running back who now works in Rozelle's office, to Tallahassee to mollify Gaither. But Young was unsuccessful, and the NFL flew Jake and his wife to New York for further talks. In the end, the NFL offered Jake $25,000 in cash, three thousand tickets to the Colts-Dolphins game, $15,000 in radio advertising for the Orange Blossom Classic, and two scholarships, each worth $1,500 as recompense for moving his game to an earlier time.

Gaither declined the offer, saying his $75,000 request was not unreasonable.

"The price was set in a realistic effort to break even," he said at the time. "Last year we drew more than thirty thousand to the game. If we played at eleven A.M. on the eleventh, we figured it would cost us fifteen thousand fans at five dollars each.

"I told them I didn't know anything about advertising, but I suspect that fifteen thousand dollars wouldn't go too far. The two scholarships were okay. Now, what am I going to do with three thousand tickets to the Dolphins-Baltimore game? I'm not in the ticket-selling business. We needed something concrete. We were not going to jeopardize our efforts and organization to accommodate the NFL. We're trying to protect FAMU.

"We scheduled this game in good faith, and we're not responsible for this boo-boo. It's the first time I've ever been criticized for taking a stand that's right. You don't have to pressure Jake to do what's right. You can't pressure Jake to do what's wrong."

Jake was not unaware of the NFL's hefty television revenues. In 1973, for instance, the league received $40 million from television rights. Of this amount, each team received about $1.5 million. In addition, the NFL received $1.5 million for each conference game and $2.75 million for the Super Bowl. Yet they refused to make an attractive offer to Florida A&M.

Newspaper editorials in Florida began urging Jake and the impenitent NFL to reach a compromise. An editorial titled "No Blackout, Please" appeared in the *Miami News* on November 18. It said in part, "Florida A&M's athletic director, Jake Gaither, is holding onto his rights to a TV blackout, understandably, since his gate stands to suffer otherwise. NFL league executives have not attempted to negotiate a settlement with Gaither to permit the telecast.

"Some sort of financial indemnity to A&M is indicated. As *Miami News* Sports Editor John Crittenden predicts, Miamians will soon be in an uproar when they realize the game won't be televised. The NFL and Florida A&M could generate untold goodwill by working out an agreement to lift the blackout."

Sportswriters urged each fan to contribute a dollar for the "Buck the Blackout" drive. Miami attorney Ellis S. Rubin wrote Gaither asking him to lift the blackout. He said he would "personally undertake a public subscription [to the Classic] in Palm Beach, Broward, Dade, and Monroe counties to sell tickets." Rubin said he would "guarantee that we will sell more tickets than the thirty thousand five hundred who attended last year's Orange Blossom Classic." Gaither never considered the offer.

Jake exacerbated the situation by telling the press—incorrectly—that a South Florida newspaper had refused to run advertisements for the Classic "because of our unreasonable stand" in not waiving the blackout ban. Actually, the sports editor of the paper in question—*The News Tribune* of Fort Pierce, Florida—said they would not give coverage to the Classic because of FAMU's position. In a letter to Roosevelt Wilson, the school's sports information director, dated December 1, 1971, the editor wrote:

Dear Mr. Wilson:

Because of your school's unreasonable stand on the television blackout of the Miami-Baltimore professional football game of Dec. 11, we will be forced to devote all our space on Sunday, Dec. 12, to coverage of the Dolphins, in order to keep our readers informed of how the game went when, in reality, they should have been able to see it on television.

Because of space limitations, we will be unable to carry any news, either before the game or after it, of the Orange Blossom Classic.

Sincerely yours,
James B. Clark, Jr.
Sports Editor

As the pressures continued to build, Gaither asked the National Collegiate Athletic Association (NCAA), a perennial sparring mate of professional football—the NCAA has consistently and unimpressively argued that the NFL seeks to harm college football—to state their position on the imbroglio. Thomas C. Hansen, assistant executive director of the NCAA, sent the following telegram to Gaither:

Telecast of Miami-Baltimore game is subject to Public Law 87-331 because the NFL commissioner's office chose to schedule the game on Saturday during college football season. The law protects high school and college football from encroachment by professional football upon two days of the week reserved by Congress for amateur football. NFL is well aware of law despite misleading statements that telecast is blocked by NCAA rule.

NFL knew law and date of your game and is to blame for scheduling Miami game in this manner, even though it is now trying to focus blame for television problems on others.

Professional football can play on any day of the week and can televise without restriction on five of seven days of the week. Despite this latitude, they continually interfere with college football and try to televise against it when, in fact, they refuse to televise their own sold-out games in their community when they play at home.*

Your famed Orange Blossom Classic deserves the full support of all football fans and most of all professional football, which has profited immeasurably from Florida A&M's splendid football program.

Gaither's pitch in the early stages of the controversy was, "I gave them [NFL] a way out, but they expected me to lose money . . . what they offered us was like throwing a bone to a dog. And the Florida A&M Rattlers are no hound dogs."

But as tension escalated, his approach was less dogmatic, even conciliatory.

"I'd like to see the Dolphins game at Baltimore Saturday on TV," he said. "I'd love to see it, but the law prohibits it. People are turning around asking Jake to be a lawbreaker. I always thought they wanted Jake to be a law-abiding citizen." He said he had always obeyed the law, even those requiring racial segregation, adding, "Nobody knows more about unfair laws than I do . . ."

In an interview with Gary Long of the Miami *Herald*, Gaither said, "Florida A and M is a member of the

*Congress enacted legislation prior to the 1973 season permitting local televising of a game if all tickets are sold out seventy-two hours before kickoff. Under pressure from Congress, which was considering lifting the ban permanently, the NFL agreed to keep the practice in effect on an experimental basis for several years. Although the law allows local stations to televise a game, the station retains the right to decide whether to televise or not.

NCAA, a great body that wields a tremendous influence. I am a lifetime trustee of the American Football Coaches Association. I am a member of the powerful NCAA TV committee. How can I, in honor, turn against the NCAA, the AFCA, and the TV committee, all of whom have fought so long to get this law? Ask the NFL to play the game on Sunday, the twelfth, then every truck driver, every cook, and every maid could see it . . . if the great NFL could change the game from Saturday to Sunday, where it should have been to start with. But that way they'd have lost [TV] money. They would sell you short, sell every fan of the Dolphins short—kick them in the pants—just to make money. And then put the blame on Jake."

The game was a hot potato and the NFL, fearing it would get burned, passed it back to the Miami Dolphins and Gaither.

"This office prepares and announces league schedules after first checking with each of the twenty-six teams as to possible conflicts," Rozelle wrote to Ellis S. Rubin, a Miami attorney. "The Orange Blossom conflict was not mentioned to us when the schedule and dates were cleared. Inasmuch as Mr. Jake Gaither, of the sponsoring institution, has in the past permitted professional telecasts in South Florida on the days of his Orange Blossom Classic, perhaps this will be possible again this year."

But Miami writers threw the potato back at the National Football League.

One columnist wrote, "The NFL schedule-maker is to blame, and the league executives were wrong not to offer

A&M a sizable payoff to lift the blackout. But the public is going to blame A&M, and that's a shame because the bricks should be thrown at the National Football League."

Pete Rozelle quickly became *persona non grata* in Miami. In an attempt to ameliorate the situation, Rozelle announced the Wednesday before the game that the NFL would sponsor a closed-circuit showing of the Baltimore-Miami game for Miami area fans. In addition to offending Gaither, who contended that the showing would violate the spirit, if not the letter, of the law, three lawsuits were filed within two days to thwart the broadcast.

One suit filed by Jesse McCray, a Miami attorney and FAMU graduate, on behalf of a Florida A&M student and the publisher of the game program, charged that the telecast would do "irreparable financial damage" to Florida A&M. United States District Judge C. Clyde Atkins, however, denied the request for a temporary injunction, saying the damage would not be irreparable "and can be compensated by money."

Another petition filed by attorneys representing Sunbeam Television Corporation, owner of the NBC affiliate in Miami (WCKT–Channel 7), sought an injunction barring Sports Action, Inc., the closed circuit company, from broadcasting the game in Miami and West Palm Beach as announced. That suit was dismissed on the grounds that the station's contract with NBC did not cover closed-circuit games.

The third suit was filed by Ellis S. Rubin, the Miami attorney who has long viewed himself as a gadfly, although the Dolphins and the NFL see him as a pest. At last count, Rubin had filed eleven lawsuits against the

Dolphins or the National Football League, or both. In addition to testifying before the Senate's Commerce Committee against the NFL's blackout policy, which has since been lifted, Rubin has filed suits to lift the blackouts, to replace the artificial turf in the Orange Bowl, and to prevent the Dolphins from including exhibition games in the season-ticket package—all of which he lost. In 1975, the Dolphins notified Rubin, a season-ticket holder since the team came to Miami in 1966, that his season tickets would not be renewed because he had cost the club more than $12,000 in legal fees to defend against his suits; Rubin is fighting that one, too.

This time, however, Rubin was representing a motel owner in Fort Lauderdale who charged that by not allowing the game to be seen on television, the NFL would effectively deny him customers, many of whom gave parties in his motel to view each Dolphin away game. In his suit against Gaither and the NFL, Rubin alleged that the Classic was not a regularly scheduled game—at least not for FAMU's opponent, which is selected late in the season—and that the game had not been announced prior to March 1 as required by Public Law 87-331.

Jake, who did not receive his subpoena until 7:00 A.M. on the day he was to appear, testified that the Orange Blossom Classic was a regular season game and that it had been announced in due time.

United States Judge Charles B. Fulton denied Rubin's motion for a hearing, which was filed on Wednesday, because it did not give FAMU adequate time to fully prepare for litigation. He said further that the motel owner had not sued for damages. Gaither thanked the judge, adding, "I'd like to invite you to our game Saturday night." The gesture was vintage Jake.

Meanwhile, Dolphin fans were still piqued at Rozelle, surmising that the Florida A&M–Dolphin debacle was an experiment for pay TV as well as yet another example of pro football's cupidity.

On the eve of the game, Rozelle issued the following statement:

There is considerable confusion, distortion and misunderstanding regarding plans to present a closed-circuit showing of the Miami Dolphin game from Baltimore tomorrow in the Miami area.

We would have much preferred to have had this game presented on free home television as with all Dolphins away games. This was not legally possible. The closed-circuit plans were substituted for two reasons and two reasons only:

1. To help accommodate the strong desire of avid Dolphin fans to view the game as it was being played and hopefully eliminate the possibility we were told existed that some might make unfair protests against the playing of the Orange Blossom Classic.

2. To permit Dolphin fans viewing the closed-circuit to indirectly contribute to a worthwhile charity—Balafonte-Tacolcy Youth Center—in the Miami area. All proceeds will be paid the charity after actual expenses, including a nominal fee rather than the normal healthy percentages of receipts being paid by contract to the promoter of the closed-circuit telecast.

It should be emphasized that the National Football League and its member clubs will receive absolutely no income from this endeavor and anyone wishing to review or audit the expenses and disbursements is free to do so.

Anyone suggesting the National Football League is con-
ducting this closed-circuit telecast as a test for future pay
telecast of teams' away games is permitting suspicions (obviously calculated in some public statements) to obscure the
facts. Such individuals are disregarding League Congressio-
nal testimony and also proposed FCC guidelines concerning
sport telecasts.

The NFL has no desire to hamper in any way Florida
A&M's conduct of the annual Orange Blossom Classic to be
played in Miami tomorrow night. It is strongly felt that anyone paying to watch the afternoon closed-circuit telecast
would have listened to the Dolphin-Colt game on radio and
perhaps further satisfied their football interest by viewing
the telecast of another college game being televised into
Miami tomorrow under NCAA auspices.

That last sentence was obviously a barb directed at the
NCAA's double-standard of not wanting the NFL to telecast in an area where a college game is being played, yet
doing the same thing themselves through their Game of
the Week on the American Broadcast Company net-
work.

At any rate, the game was switched to Baltimore,
but the beleagured Rozelle ran into another lawsuit,
this one filed by a group of merchants whose busi-
nesses are near Memorial Stadium. They charged that
a game played two weeks before Christmas would cre-
ate traffic congestion, causing them "irreparable loss of
sales, income and customers" during the prime of the
holiday season. They lost their suit and the game was
played. The irony in the controversy is that fans in neither home town got to see the game televised, Miami
because of the federal law and Baltimore because of

the NFL blackout rule then in effect.

Baltimore won the game 14–3, as the thirty-eight-year-old Johnny Unitas played one of the better games in his declining years, completing 16 of 19 passes, including 10 consecutive passes during one stretch. The Miami rushing game, which had been averaging 182 yards per game, was limited to 101 yards. The Dolphin offense, which had been averaging 24 points a game, failed to score a touchdown.

About an hour after the pro game ended, Florida A&M, having one of its worst seasons in the history of the school with 5 wins and 5 losses, defeated Kentucky State, 27–9, in the Orange Blossom Classic. Freshman halfback James Rackley scored 3 touchdowns and rushed for 155 yards, ending the season with 791 yards rushing, just 29 yards shy of Willie Galimore's 1956 school record (Rackley broke the record in 1974 with 881 yards).

FAMU alumni went out of their way to drum up support for the game. About twenty-six thousand persons attended, most of them black; thirty-one thousand had attended the previous year. They were all happy after the game and one woman was heard to say, "Tonight, God was on our side. He knew we were not treated right and He did something about it. God made ugly, but He don't like it."

If God was in Miami that night, chances are that He didn't attend the closed-circuit showing. Only about fifteen hundred did, all of them mere mortals. The Dolphins were able to come back from their defeat the following week, however, by defeating the Green Bay Packers while the Colts were being upset by the New England Patriots. The Dolphins went on to the Super Bowl that year, where they lost to Dallas, 24–3, thus becoming the first and only team to play in a Super Bowl game without scoring a touchdown.

11

Desegregated, Demoted, Defunct

The Jake Gaither farm system, the well-oiled machine that had consistently produced fresh talent for Florida A&M since 1945, ground to a gradual halt in the late 1960s. The machine stopped not because of crop failure, but because it became clogged by desegregation, which was supposed to be the panacea for a myriad of social problems afflicting blacks.

It is as ironic as it is sad that blacks were forced to attend predominantly black schools because America, for the most part, did not move with any speed, let alone all deliberate speed, to remove all vestiges of discrimination and segregation. Yet when it appears, superficially at least, that many of these barriers are falling as a result of increased desegregation, it is the black schools and educators who seem to be suffering most because of this belated acceptance of blacks as human beings.

Of paramount concern to Gaither, and others similiarly situated, is the fact that under desegregation plans ordered by the Department of Health, Education and Welfare, the black secondary schools are being closed or converted to junior high schools. More often than not, the black role models—teachers, coaches, and principals—are also being displaced. Black colleges, already seeing what had been a rich pool of black talent to choose from dissipate (the black high schools), are also faced with competition on the college level. The white institutions of higher learning that once turned their backs on Afro-Americans are now getting the best black athletes for their own teams with the aid of wealthy alumni, bloated budgets that approach the national debt in size and, in some instances, illegal financial enticements. Meanwhile, Gaither and other black college coaches have been left on the sidelines, forgotten or largely ignored. While there is no denying that these black coaches would rather get these same athletes themselves, as they did in the past, the problem runs deeper than mere selfishness.

"Here they find a better social life and a more satisfying comradeship," Gaither says. "The entire faculty is interested in the welfare of the boy. He gets a lot of personal attention, and we follow him all through life. I feel obligated to make sure that when a boy graduates, he gets a job. My boys have gone on to coach at all but four or five of the black high schools in Florida. They can't get this kind of attention at white schools."

The point was expressed more succinctly several years ago when a black, about to graduate from a large Northern university, approached Gaither about a coaching job at a meeting of the American Football Coaches Association.

Asked the student, "You mean to tell me no whites go to your school?"

Gaither replied, "Yes."

"Are most of the teachers black?"

"Yes, they are."

"Are all the students black?"

"Yes."

"Then why should I go to your school?"

"In the first place, you're black. You were born black and you're going to die black. Nine times out of ten, you're going to marry a black woman. You're going to live in a black neighborhood. Your friends from this day until the day you die are going to be black. You got to work with them and you're going to live with them and you're going to die with them. Don't kid yourself, those white classmates that you see are not going to be your lifelong friends. That's probably the last time you're going to see them. You need to go to a black school to learn something about the people you got to live and die with."

The student applied to Florida A&M later for a coaching job.

HEW statistics present yet an even stronger case for the black college. Although only 118 of the nation's 1457 four-year nonspecialized institutions of higher education are predominantly black, those schools graduate about the same number of undergraduates—about 25,000 annually —as white institutions, even though they enroll only 25 to 30 percent of black college students. Moreover, black colleges have produced about 60 percent of the nation's high-level black civil servants, 74 percent of the black Ph.D.s, 75 percent of the black military officers, and 80 percent of the nation's black physicians.

Most of the black civil and human rights leaders were educated at black colleges: W. E. B. DuBois, a founding member of the National Association for the Advancement of Colored People; Booker T. Washington, the former Tuskegee Institute president; Whitney Young of the Urban League; John Lewis and Stokely Carmichael of the

Student Nonviolent Co-ordinating Committee; Jesse Jackson, president of PUSH (People United to Save Humanity), Georgia legislator Julian Bond; Mrs. Margaret Bush Wilson, chairman of the NAACP board of directors; the Rev. Ralph Abernathy and Dr. Martin Luther King, Jr., of the Southern Christian Leadership Conference.

Many of the large white universities, prodded by litigation, affirmative action programs, and a HEW threat to withhold federal funds if they did not desegregate, reluctantly began opening up their schools and athletic programs to blacks in the late 1960s. Much of the increased activity can be attributed to Title VI of the Civil Rights Act of 1964, section 601 which states: "No person in the United States shall, on the grounds of race, color, creed, or national origin, be excluded from the participation in, be denied benefits of, or be subjected to discrimination under any program receiving Federal financial assistance."

Still, the road has not been easy.

In 1965, Gene Stallings, the bucolic coach of Texas A&M said, "I've got nothing against the Negro athlete, but I don't believe he fits into our plans right now. What we need is a team that will work and pull and fight together and really get a feeling of oneness. We need to be a complete unit. I don't believe we could accomplish this with a Negro on the squad."

Stalling's former boss, Alabama's Bear Bryant, who for years coached lily-white teams himself,* acknowledged

---

*The University of Alabama and Druid High School, a predominantly black institution, are both located in Tuscaloosa, Alabama. Druid has long been regarded as an incubator of exceptionally talented athletes—such as Speedy Dun-

the black athlete's contribution to his squads in his 1974 autobiography, *Bear Bryant: The Hard Life and Good Times of Alabama's Coach Bryant.*

With more hindsight than foresight, Bryant observed, "The big difference is that kids are a lot more knowledgeable, and that's no revelation. More knowledgeable about money, about life—about everything. And I hate to admit it, but football doesn't mean as much to them. All I had was football, and I hung on as though it were life or death, which it was. And up until about 10 years ago that's the way life was for most of our players. But *now.* Their mamas and papas can make more on relief than we could working. All of them came from something, or 90 per cent of them.

"The ones who will consistently suck their guts up and stick by you now are the blacks, because they don't have anything to go back to. And I've come to appreciate that in the last few years. Bo Schembechler of Michigan told me once, 'A black won't ever quit on you,' and I got to thinking the way it had been for me, and he was right. Because I didn't have any place to go, either."

But to Bryant and other Southern white coaches, it was not a question of who would stick with them. On the contrary, it was *realpolitik*—they needed blacks to win games against teams that showed no reluctance toward playing Afro-Americans. As Neil Amdur wrote in the December 11, 1969, *New York Times:*

"It is the large white universities that are siphoning off

can of the San Diego Chargers and Washington Redskins and Dave Washington of the San Francisco 49ers—yet Bryant never attempted to recruit blacks in his community.

the rich black talent once recruited by Gaither, Eddie Robinson at Grambling and John Merritt of Tennessee State. And it is these same white schools, for the most part, which are helped by tougher integration codes, by junior college farm systems, red-shirting, bowl trips, and the esthetic campus dreams that disillusioned blacks later protest as evil and unjust."

Competition from larger white institutions was only half of Gaither's problem; the other half was that the last two decades brought a dismanteling of the dual school system in the South, a system in which 99.999 percent of the black students attended all-black institutions. Today, less than 9 percent of Southern blacks attend all-black high schools. Slightly more than half of the black students are enrolled in predominantly black schools. Roughly two-thirds of black students in the North, West, and border states remain in predominantly black schools.

Significantly, many students who had been going directly from all-black high schools in the South to all-black colleges are now moving from racially mixed schools to racially mixed colleges. Below are HEW figures documenting the pace of desegregation in the eleven Southern states, the thirty-two Northern and Western States, and the six Border states and the District of Columbia.

BLACKS IN MAJORITY WHITE SCHOOLS

	U.S.	South	Border & D.C.	North & West
1968–69	23.4%	18.4%	28.4%	27.6%
1970–71	33.1%	40.3%	28.7%	27.6%
1972–73	36.3%	46.3%	31.8%	28.3%

BLACKS IN ALL-BLACK SCHOOLS

	U.S.	South	Border & D.C.	North & West
1968–69	39.7%	68.0%	25.2%	12.3%
1970–71	14.0%	14.4%	24.1%	11.7%
1972–73	11.2%	8.7%	23.6%	10.9%

SCHOOL DESEGREGATION, 1954–74
Blacks in schools with whites in 11 Southern states

1954–55	.001%	1964–65	2.25%
1955–56	.115%	1965–66	6.1%
1956–57	.144%	1966–67	15.9%
1957–58	.151%	1967–68	NA
1958–59	.132%	1968–69	32.0%
1959–60	.160%	1969–70	NA
1960–61	.162%	1970–71	85.6%
1961–62	.241%	1971–72	90.8%
1962–63	.453%	1972–73	91.3%
1963–64	1.17%	1973–74	NA

Source: Office for Civil Rights, Department of HEW

The swift acceleration of school desegregation has produced a corresponding increase of school desegregation complaints by black students and teachers, many of them apparently justified. B. Drummond Ayres, Jr., writing in the May 13, 1974, *New York Times,* observed:

"No matter how successful the desegregation has been, however, whites and blacks still tend to go their separate ways once out of the classroom and off the playing field. There is minimal mingling in the lunchroom, at the senior prom (if it has not been canceled).

"Most integrated schools have begun 'tracking' or 'ability grouping' their better students into accelerated courses, a procedure that sometimes resegregates whites and blacks.

"Where black and white systems have been merged, black principals and teachers have sometimes been demoted or dismissed.

"Where discipline is a major desegregation problem, black students often are punished more severely and more frequently than whites."

The National Education Association (NEA) and the Mississippi Teachers Association, in an *amicus curiae* brief filed in support of three black teachers and an assistant principal who were fired in 1970 by the Columbus, Mississippi, school board, stated that racial discrimination in the dismissal and demotion of black educators is still widespread. The brief, filed in the fall of 1973, said that data compiled from three-fourths of the districts in Alabama, Georgia, Louisiana, and Mississippi disclosed a decline of more than twenty-five hundred black teachers between 1968, the year immediately prior to meaningful desegregation, and 1972; during that same period, 3,387 white teachers were added to the payrolls.

Statistics from 70 percent of the districts in Florida, Georgia, Louisiana, and Mississippi showed that between 1968 and 1972, those districts eliminated almost 20 percent of their black principalships while increasing their white principalships by 6 percent. The education groups argued that black educators were removed despite a 1971 court order stipulating that teacher dismissals must be made on the basis of reasonable nondiscriminatory standards.

But Jake Gaither needs no one to tell him that black schools, principals, and coaches are an endangered species, about to become as extinct as the dinosaur.

"Integration has just about eliminated the black coach," he says. "I used to have a lot of my boys in high school jobs. After integration, most of them became assistant coaches or rubdown boys. They've been phased out."

He says that in a real sense, the marginal black student has been phased out, too.

"I think on the high school level, segregation will gradually fade out completely," he says. "But on the college level we don't want it. We've had 100 years of discrimination and unequal facilities. We can't overcome that overnight. A kid would have to be Superman . . . just take off out of the window and fly . . . to overcome that. We're going to need black schools, most of which don't have as high academic standards as older institutions, to bridge that gap. It took this long to open that gap, and it'll take time to close it.

"Fundamentally, I think the biggest weakness in integration for my people is that the white teacher doesn't give a damn. The one thing that we didn't anticipate when we were fighting for integration—we took for granted the idea that if a child happened to get under a white teacher, that teacher was going to give him every chance to get an education and would be just as concerned about his getting an education as he would be for white kids. That's where we were wrong. When we have whites teaching black kids, the tendancy is to put blacks in the back of the room, let them play cards all day, or let them stay out of school all day—as long as they don't disturb the other kids. Our kids are not getting as good an education as they got before integration. Blacks had black teachers and coaches telling them, 'You got to go to college. You got to be somebody.' The white teacher doesn't care whether he goes or not. Also, the blacks are losing opportunities for leadership—to be class president, student body president, or newspaper editor. In Pensacola they had trouble over wanting the black students to sing 'Dixie.' "

As a result of desegregation, Gaither says, his task of recruiting the best athletes became difficult, if not impossible.

"When you recruit a boy, you got to know the coach," he explains. "You got to know the quality of the opposition. Here is the difficulty we're running into now in recruiting. If possible, the white coach is going to send his boys to his friends. His friends may be in Kansas, his friends may be in Illinois, his friends may be anywhere. For the longest time, Southern schools wouldn't take blacks, so coaches sent them to other conferences. The coach's loyalty is to his friend, not me. You got to know the coach. You got to know his fairness, his honesty, and his ability to evaluate a black boy. There is usually so much difference between the native ability of blacks and whites playing football—I won't say native ability, I'll say ability —the black is faster, he's bigger, and he's stronger. I heard about a kid down in South Florida. The white coach called me up and said, 'We've got a terrific boy down here—he's an end.' He said, 'Coach, I want you to take him.' The next day the black coach called me, and I said, 'What about John Jones over at the white high school?' He said, 'Coach, he's just mediocre. He couldn't make the team over here, so he went over there. He couldn't even make our squad, but over there he was a star.'

"So I ran into that situation—the white coach's inability to make a comparative analysis of a good black boy because he was faster. What may be terrific speed for him, may be very mediocre speed when compared to other blacks. Some years ago, Bill Peterson over at FSU said, 'Jake, I never had a back who could run the hundred in less than 11.5' and I said, 'Bill, I don't think there's been a year that I didn't have five or six boys who could run the hundred-yard dash in under ten seconds.' There was one time when I had Bobby Hayes, who ran 9.1, Eugene White, a 9.4; and Robert Paremore, who did 9.3. That was my kick return team—a 9.1, a 9.4, and a 9.3. I've had boys like Bob Hayes, Hewritt Dixon, and Al Denson on the same team. Now, today's great athlete, I couldn't beg, borrow, or steal, but the white school could."

Hansel Tookes, Jake's successor as athletic director at FAMU, echos Gaither's sentiments.

"We're lucky to get the third choice," he says dourly. "If the black athlete is gifted mentally and physically, Georgia Tech or one of these real fine schools will get him. And if he's gifted athletically and has average academic ability, then that middle school, like Kansas, will get him. Then if he's a great athlete and he's stupid—nothing on the ball academically—then Southern or Texas Southern will come in and say, 'Man, you don't have to worry about a test.' Now you come to the mediocre guy who doesn't have any sense either. *No* academic ability, and the coaches want to peddle him off on us. The only guy who might be a superstar for us is the guy who was a late bloomer—he hadn't showed anything in high school."

John Merritt of Tennessee State, like all black college coaches, dislikes the exploitation he sees going on in predominantly white universities. And he laments the fact that the black athlete is unable, or unwilling, to recognize this fact.

"We see three things happening," Merritt says. "Number one, blacks still can't say no to whites—that's number one. Number two, so many blacks still believe that if it's white, it's right and, number three, blacks are still so poor that they are susceptible to selling their birthrights—they just sell themselves out to whites. So those are your three basic reasons that we're catching hell now getting the top black athletes.

"And the whites are ruining them characterwise. You see Franco Harris and Oscar Robertson—the great ones— but twice as many blacks didn't make it out of school. It is only accidental, by chance, that we succeed [in white colleges]. I tell those who go to white schools, 'You're not a student, you're an entertainer. You're entertaining the other students, alumni, and fans.' "

To counterbalance his dwindling pool of athletes, Gaither decided to do what he had for years only joked about—recruit white players. But from the outset, Jake believed—and his experience later confirmed—that he would not make much headway.

"We don't want a white boy just to say we have one," he stated. "They have to make the team like anyone else. Chances are they'd have to be superior even to make the squad. But they'll get a fair shake from Jake." He described another problem he encounters.

"Many times after we notify a high school coach we're coming to his school on a recruiting mission, and he'll bring out only his black boys," Gaither says. "The assumption is that we only want the black players, but that's not true and it puts us in an embarrassing situation."

Florida A&M signed its first white scholarship athlete, Rufus Brown, to a grant-in-aid in 1968. Brown, a five-foot nine-inch 205-pound All-Conference guard at Martin County High in Stuart, Florida, was kind of a white Jackie Robinson.

"To tell the truth, I didn't even think about that," he said, referring to his becoming the first non-black scholarship athlete at FAMU. "A four year grant-in-aid, all expenses paid for tuition, room and board, laundry—you can't beat that. I get a free education out of it." Then, tongue-in-cheek, he added, "It was the school that offered the most."

It was also the only offer he received.

Brown was also awarded a racially inspired nickname, Rap Brown. Family problems forced Brown to withdraw from FAMU later. An even uglier problem forced the withdrawal of another football player who broke the color barrier at FAMU. Joe Jewett, a freshman place-kicker from Miami, learned to his dismay that racism comes in all colors—including black. He quit in the middle of the 1970 season, apparently because a group of blacks wantonly harassed and threatened him. Jewett had a withered left arm, and was taunted by such remarks as:

"Hey whitey, what happened to your arm? Somebody step on it?"

"What's the matter, boy, not good enough for Florida State?"

"Well, look what we got here: White Power!"

Jewett finally packed his belongings and left. It was unfortunate that the young man left, because he was a credit to his race—the human race.

"You can take only so much of it," he explained later. "I finally left. My relationship with the team was one of the best I ever ran into. I got along with the coaches real well, and the players were just great to me. I used to talk over my problems with a player they called Blue Pete. I never did learn his last name, but he would always ask how I was doing in class. But I never let him or the other players know about the difficulties I was having because I didn't want to bring any trouble on them. They're a great bunch of guys."

Jewett said his roommate, a black, supported his decision to withdraw. "His name is Henry Lawrence," Jewett says. "He's real nice and we got along fine. He agreed that what I was going through was bad and that he wouldn't have taken it either."

Gaither says he doesn't blame the player for leaving and says that he disapproves of the conduct, yet Jewett experienced what had been a way of life for many blacks in the South.

"He was a fine young boy and everyone on the team got along with him real well," Jake says. "Actually, he was the first white player we've had who could have helped us. He was a fine kicker, and we lost a couple of games after he left that we could have won if he had been kicking for us.

"But when he would sit in the school cafeteria, a small

group of our students, who are militants, would stand over him and say, 'Now what are we going to do with him?' Finally the kid couldn't take any more and he went home."

By no stretch of the imagination was Jewett an exceptional athlete—fair, but not exceptional. And Gaither concedes that he doesn't really expect FAMU to recruit the top white athlete, although there have been several whites on the squad. Like Jewett, however, they were nothing to write home about.

"It'll be a long time, if ever, before black schools will get good white athletes," Gaither says. "If he's good, the white schools will get him. The boys that we get will be the boys they don't want. I think we might as well forget looking for that blue chipper or super athlete among the white boys. But I think that if we have white boys in our communities who want to attend our schools, they should be given every opportunity to attend our schools; they should be given every opportunity to participate in every activity of the school on the same level as any black student."

What is the fate of black intercollegiate athletics? Or, more important, what is the fate of black colleges?

Since hindsight is always 20/20, the answer to those questions may be provided by future scholars. But there are compelling reasons, too many to be listed in this space, for the retention of black institutions. Meanwhile, black educators must begin reversing the brain drain—and muscle drain—that is the result of desegregation.

Athleticly, especially in football, it appears that black colleges have no alternative except to follow the lead of

Grambling State University and a few other black colleges that now play at least some of their "home" games in such distant cities as New York, the District of Columbia, Detroit, Chicago, Los Angeles, and Houston. Three advantages for doing so immediately come to mind: One, it provides opportunities to showcase the school's talent across the country, thus making it easier to recruit players. Two, it neutralizes recruiters from white universities who charge that only by attending their schools will black athletes get ample travel opportunities. And, three, it augments lagging income at athletic events.*

Florida A&M played Howard University during the 1975 season in Philadelphia's Veterans Stadium and seems to be moving toward more big-city exposure under Tooke's tenure as athletic director.

Academically, as evidenced in statistics cited earlier in this chapter, there is a clear and persuasive case for preserving black colleges, partly because of their past achievements, and partly because of the exceptional job they continue to do today.

Any efforts to save predominantly black institutions of higher learning may benefit, if inadvertently, from what may be slowly developing as a trend toward resegregation through the establishment of white "private academies," staunch resistance to court-ordered busing, and the increasingly black inner city public schools. Presumably, black students, having again attended predominantly black high schools, will find it easy, even preferable, to

---

*Still another innovation, also pioneered by Grambling, is showing black football games on television. The future benefits to black schools can be substantial.

matriculate at black colleges.

It may be too soon to say with certainty that racial segregation, particularly in the Deep South, is about to rise again, to borrow a famous phrase, but there are unmistakable signs that are, at the very least, troubling. For example, almost 10 percent of the South's school-aged pupils are attending thirty-five hundred lily-white private academies throughout the region. Without question, these facilities are as Southern as Dixie. About one-sixth of Charlotte, North Carolina's white pupils are enrolled in such institutions and about half of the white students in Jackson, Mississippi, are enrolled in the academies. In Memphis, Tennessee, about twenty-five thousand white students have transferred to private schools.

But black colleges may win the battle and lose the war.

There is a possibility that Florida A&M, which shares residency in Tallahassee with predominantly white Florida State University, may be absorbed by the larger institution, since both are state-supported. A similar fate threatens other black state-supported institutions located in the same town with white state universities, some of which were only recently built. For example, Tennessee State and the University of Tennessee at Nashville are in the same city. So are Southern University and LSU—and Alabama State and the newly-built Auburn University at Montgomery.

At least five formerly black colleges—Bluefield State, Lincoln University in Missouri, Bowie State, Delaware State, and Kentucky State—have white enrollments exceeding or approaching 50 percent. Additionally, three others—Prairie View A&M, Maryland State College, and

Arkansas AM&N—have already been absorbed into the statewide—i.e., white—educational systems.

So, black colleges, which sprang from the seeds of a dual education system, now find themselves fighting dual battles—against an attempt by some white institutions to sap their traditional supply of athletes and students, on one side, and efforts by some state officials to consolidate the historically black college with larger white institutions, on the other. If the black colleges fail to win both battles, it may be described as moot whether the traditionally black college can continue to attract black students. It will be moot because there won't be any black colleges left.

12

The Power Lover

The urge for power is as great as the urge for sex.

—JAKE GAITHER

To those who have worked or played for Jake Gaither, there have always been three ways of doing things: the right way, the wrong way, and Jake's way. To Jake, his way *was* the right way. Naturally, the attendant problem with such an attitude is that Gaither has often been perceived as obdurate. Although there is unquestioned unanimity on his success on the field, there is less than universal agreement on Jake Gaither, the man.

Gaither is seen by some as the creator of a paragon that should be emulated by future generations; others view him as an excellent coach, but a Neanderthal whose views and modus operandi clearly belong in another era, not this one. Surprisingly, the most biting criticism of Gaither comes from blacks, the very group he is credited with uplifting. Whites, on the other hand, have invariably praised him. Bill Kastelz, sports editor of the *Jacksonville Times-Union,* calls Gaither "the man I consider the greatest Negro I've ever known in the world of sports." Another writer quotes a Southern redneck as saying, "Jake is the only nigger I ever wish was a white man." Jake has his ardent black defenders as well, and the aforementioned is not to suggest that respect for Gaither is limited to whites.

Still, most of the criticism has come from blacks who see Gaither as an Uncle Tom, or an Oreo—black on the outside, but white on the inside. The reason for criticism varies, but much of it focuses on what is perceived as Jake's reluctance to protest segregation and his courting of segregationists. Critics charge that while other blacks were actively fighting all forms of discrimination, Jake remained curiously aloof, at times serving as an apologist for segregation.

Typical of Gaither's thinking is his explanation of why black and white teams had been forbidden by state officials from playing each other until recently.

"The Board of Regents gave us permission only in recent years," he says. "We couldn't play the game unless they gave us permission. A few years ago they told Dr. [President George W.] Gore that it would be perfectly alright. They were being cautious; no governor wanted to assume responsibility for something happening. They wanted to keep peace and tranquility in Florida. We hadn't had any riots or upheavals like they had in other sections of the country. It wasn't that they didn't want to have the game; they were afraid of the repercussions that might have come. When the atmosphere was favorable for it, they said go ahead with it. Now, there is no question about it. I don't think it was bitterness or strife or rancor that caused them to do that. I think it was a precautionary measure. They didn't want to take a chance. That's what I really believe."

There was one report in a South Florida newspaper in the mid-fifties that described a confrontation in Del Ray Beach between that city's blacks and whites. The trouble started when blacks wanted to use the city's beach. Jake was sent down as an emissary of the governor to persuade blacks that, in the interest of harmony, they should agree to use a swimming pool rather than the beach, a proposal that was soundly rejected.

That didn't sit too well with Gaither's critics.

Also irritating to them has been Jake's insistence on using the word *colored* or *Negro* to describe Americans of African descent. A poll conducted in the mid-sixties by *Jet* magazine, the black weekly, disclosed that most African descendants prefer being called black. Second on the list was the word *Afro-American.* Even to this day, Gaither only occasionally uses the term *black* when referring to Afro-Americans.*

"I hate the terms *black* and *white,"* he explains. "You will hear me use *Negro* a lot or *colored,* but I'm forced more or less to use the terms *black* and *white.* I hate it. I want, as much as possible, to be considered an American citizen with all the rights and privileges that go with American citizenship, and I think the quicker we can get away from differentiating—black here, white there—and just say *American,* the better."

And while Jake has to some extent refused to criticize

---

*To avoid distracting the reader, in this book the word *black* or *Afro-American* has been substituted for *Negro* or *colored* in Gaither's quotes.

whites, he has shown no hesitancy to criticize blacks, often generalizing to the point that his conclusions exceed the supporting evidence.

"When we arrive, we have our butts up on our shoulder and say, 'I am somebody,' " Gaither says matter-of-factly. "If you've ever seen *Cabin in the Skies,* the black hit about winning the sweepstakes, the first thing the man did was buy a Cadillac. He went down the street throwing away dollar bills. We can't take success with modesty. We brag. We think we're better than we are."

At least Gaither concedes there is a reason for what he describes as this typical behavior.

"We are not accustomed to it," he says. "We haven't had the chance to organize and to manage and to administer big business. It's not because we don't have the ability. You don't think bankers were born overnight. Lewis State Bank here is the oldest bank in Florida. The president's name is Lewis. The president before him was named Lewis. Old man Lewis got three sons working in that bank, and when he passes on, one of his sons will take over. They've been well-to-do for ages. How many blacks are in that position? So being big and having money doesn't faze him. But take a ragged-butt black and put him in a position of authority and he becomes the worst tyrant in the world. He wants to make everybody catch hell, like he caught hell."

And there is also the subject of Gaither's flippant characterization of his African ancestry. In a speech before a predominantly white audience in New York he remarked, "I love America. Oh, they tell me that my home is in Africa. But I want to tell you one thing: I'm not a bit homesick."

Does all of this mean, then, that Gaither is indeed an Uncle Tom? Some say yes, some say no, and others say it was simply *quid pro quo*.

"If he had taken a radical stand, he wouldn't have been able to get a lot of things he got," says Al Frazier, a former All-America halfback. "It was political expediency—Jake was playing a role."

Adds Hansel E. Tookes, the present athletic director, "Jake caught hell from both sides. He tried to act in such a way that he wouldn't antagonize the whites who really controlled a lot of things. Then, by doing this, he couldn't satisfy the black elements. He's done some things that he's been criticized for, but to him it was the best thing to do."

Jake attributes his present attitudes on race to his past. At Knoxville College, which was operated by the Presbyterian church, he had only three black teachers in his eight years there (prep school and college). And although he was later to become famous as a coach of a black school, he has never played under a black coach in his life. More important, when he was given up for dead after suffering two malignant brain tumors, a white surgeon operated on him. "Now, how can I hate those people?" he asks rhetorically.

But there is also a pragmatic basis for his decision to work within the system, however painful.

"I am a citizen of the United States of America," he explains. "Everything that I have, everything that I am, everything that I hope to be, I got in this country. I had to fight like hell to get it. Nobody knows the shortcomings of this democracy any more than I do. But I made up in my mind that I'm going to live under it. I'm going to live in the South—I've never lived anywhere else. And I'm going to fight like hell to realize first-class citizenship. Now in obtaining first-class citizenship in America, I got sense enough to know that I cannot live alone.

"When I look around me, and I see all the money is centralized in the hand of the white man—he controls the bank, he controls law enforcement, he controls the courts of justice, he controls the running of the United States of America—the only way in the world I can progress as a citizen of this country is somehow I've got to work out a relationship with the man in control."

Finally, Gaither cites the religious reason for adopting his approach. He says, "The basis of the Christian religion is conversion. The basis of my life is Christianity and the Good Book. That's my guide; I don't know a better one. I want to live the good life and I want to do the right thing. When Christ left this earth, they said, 'How will Your work be carried on?' He said, 'Through My disciples.' He was constantly trying to convert. The history of the Christian religion is one of conversion. So, the persecuted victim is being called upon. What we've been trying to do with the Southern white man for years is convert him. He's been heading down this road for years."

Jake's eyes light up and he grins broadly.

"I'm reminded of the joke about the white boy who could speak to his father in hell. The boy said, 'You know, I'm really giving these niggers hell, just like you told me. I'm really giving them hell.' The man said, 'Take it easy on them. You know the fireman down here is a nigger.'"

Gaither lets out an infectious laugh before continuing.

"My point is this," he says. "Here's a guy who has been going down the road giving us hell. The Ku Klux Klan—

he's been giving us hell. The conditions of the South got worldwide publicity—in the newspapers, on the radio and television. And this made the South very self-conscious. They're a proud people and they knew what was said was true. Something said to him, 'This is not right. You know you've been wrong all the time.' So he turned around and said, 'I'm going to do better to those people.' Conversion—the basis of Christianity.

"Now, some blacks say, 'I don't want your help.' They talk about the hell they gave us forty or fifty years ago instead of saying, 'I'm glad you're converted. Now we can work together.' This is the way I feel: When he's turning around and coming back, grab him by the arm and pull him on back with you. If you ever do that, you got yourself a friend. He'll stick by you come hell or high water. We got the Southern white man turned around. There isn't a place in Tallahassee that you can't go. I know it's money, but a lot of it is genuine conversion.

"I just can't hate everything white and love everything black. I don't care if they're blacker than the ace of spades or white as snow. I realize that there are lousy ones in our race and theirs. I want to be associated with the good ones."

Aside from the religious considerations, there were other tangible benefits to be obtained from Gaither's approach. His seemingly docile public posture aided him in the eyes of whites because he posed no threat. He was accommodating to the point that seating in the early years of the Orange Blossom Classic was segregated.

Jake cultivated each incoming governor, many of them avowed segregationists, and this acquaintanceship has had its advantages. For example, Gaither declares that the only reason he got raises in his years at Florida A&M —he earned $2,400 when he started in 1945 and about $22,000 when he retired in 1973—was because the state's governors gave them to him. Asked why his salary, which was about $10,000 a year less than his counterpart at Florida State, was not higher, he replies bitterly.

"It was not because the state wouldn't pay it. It was because the nigger presidents wouldn't recommend it. Every president that I've had—and I've had four— refused to give me a decent salary. No one can override him [the college president] but the governor. Our presidents have been so jealous that they would not recommend a decent salary. Every grade I got in salary was given by governors. I could have gotten any salary the president recommended. The whites wanted me to have it; and what I got finally was what they gave me, not him. That's been the story."

His ties with Governor Farris Bryant in 1962 also worked to his advantage. Bob Hayes's scheduled entry in the National AAU championships in Walnut, California, would have been canceled because FAMU didn't have the funds if Bryant had not offered $1000 of his personal funds to pay for the trip. Gaither accepted the check and returned $500 that was unused. Hayes won the race.

Still another governor came to Hayes's rescue when it appeared that the probation board was hesitating on recommending a pardon for Hayes. Gaither telephoned Governor Haydon Burns, arranged a meeting, and the matter was soon resolved—in Hayes's favor.

Except during the Reconstruction Era, until recently

the governors and every other political officeholder in
Florida were white. In both the post-Civil War period and
today, most of the nation's black public officials are in the
South. The early breakthroughs were in the North: John
Mercer Langston became the nation's first black elected
official in 1855 when he was voted clerk of Brownhelm
Township in Loraine County, Ohio; in 1866 Charles L.
Mitchell and Edward G. Walker were elected to the Mas-
sachusetts House of Representatives, thus becoming the
first blacks to serve in a state legislature.

But the higher positions were held by Southern blacks. ·
In 1868 Oscar J. Dunn was elected lieutenant governor of
Louisiana, and two years later, Hiram Revels was elected
to fill the unexpired U.S. Senate term of Jefferson Davis,
the former head of the Confederacy. In South Carolina,
Joseph H. Rainey was elected to the United States House
of Representatives in 1870, a feat he was to repeat four
times.

Those and other gains were nullified through a series of
extralegal and technically legal manueverings on the part
of Southern whites: Southern states amended their consti-
tutions and imposed poll taxes, educational requirements,
and literacy tests that posed such questions as, "How
many bubbles are there in a bar of soap?" and passed
other measures designed to disenfranchise blacks. The
states also passed the "Grandfather Clause," which
waived the voting restrictions for any person whose
ancestors were eligible to vote as of January 1, 1867. Since
blacks were not allowed to vote then, the law effectively
denied blacks access to the polls. Coupled with lynching
and intimidation, these measures served to reestablish

white supremacy in the South.

Today, a century after Reconstruction, more than half of the nation's black elected officials hold office in the South. The Joint Center for Political Studies, an independent organization in the District of Columbia that monitors black political growth, reported in late 1976 that more than thirty-nine hundred blacks held elective office in forty-six states and the District of Columbia. There were as of then, one U.S. Senator, seventeen members in the House of Representatives, two lieutenant governors, one secretary of state, a state treasurer, 276 state legislators, and two state superintendents of public instruction. Seven of the ten states with the most elected officials are in the South. Sixty-one percent of the black mayors and 44 percent of the black legislators are in the South. Overall, 57 percent—which is about the same percentage of blacks in the region as a whole—hold office in seventeen Southern states. Blacks represent less than 1 percent of all elected officials, however.

The growing number of black officials can be attributed to passage of the 1965 Voting Rights Act. Until then, whites were firmly in control, and it was with those whites in power that Gaither made his alliances, for which he has been criticized.

Undoubtedly, some of Gaither's actions and statements can be interpreted to show that he was less than assertive in helping bring about social, political, and economic advances for blacks. Equally true, however, is that there are other experiences and statements that show that he was neither docile nor apathetic toward the problems of his fellow blacks.

His readiness to come to the defense of black colleges and educators, for example, comes close to matching the fervor of Thomas Paine. For example: "There's no doubt about it, a lot of kids get better facilities at these [desegregated] schools. Some have better teachers, some do not. Not all white teachers are perfect. But they've taken the best black teachers and put them in the white schools and the worst white teachers have been placed in the black schools."

Another example: "Our kids are not getting as good an education as they did before integration. Blacks had black teachers and coaches telling them, 'You got to go to college. You got to be somebody.' The white teacher doesn't care whether he goes or not."

And there were times when Jake's actions spoke loudest of all.

One day in the early 1950s, Jake and Pete Griffin, his top assistant, were en route to Midtown, Ohio, to attend a coaching clinic. The two had driven all night. When they spotted a roadside dinner about 6:00 A.M., they parked and went inside to eat breakfast. After sitting there for several minutes, the two men noticed that persons entering the diner after them were being served first. Gaither and Griffin decided not to reach any premature conclusions and decided to wait a while longer. When it was blatantly obvious what was happening, Gaither asked the waitress, "Madam, would you serve us?" The waitress was speechless, moving her mouth in vain. Gaither asked, "Are you trying to tell me that you can't serve me because I'm black?" By this time, the manager emerged from the back and said, "You can eat in the kitchen." Rising from his seat, Gaither replied, "I don't eat in anyone's kitchen." He and Pete stormed out.

Jake still teases Pete about the incident, which was repeated on numerous occasions as they traveled throughout the country. "Pete, this is your state," Gaither jokes. "Hell, I wouldn't have made this mistake in Florida."

Gaither says that even had he taken more forthright stands, he still would have been criticized by members of the black community. He says that's one of the hazards any successful black must live with.

"I've figured it out," he says, removing two whiskey bottles from a closet in his home.

"Take this bottle. Right down here in the base of this bottle are all the blacks," he says, pointing to the base. Moving his finger upward, he says, "Right up here represents leadership—this represents accomplishments. This represents getting ahead. This represents success. Now, all my people are down here trying to get up through that little narrow funnel because our chances of success are so narrow; we have such a narrow field in which to operate. Up until five years ago, school teachers, ministers, a few lawyers, a few doctors were about the only areas in which blacks had a chance to get to the top, like that narrow bottle. And all those people were trying to get up through that bottle. You'd almost get to the top, they'd grab you and try to pull you back down—'You got my spot. I got to get up there.' It's like a house is on fire and everybody's trying to get out."

Gaither says whites can rise to the top, then move into other fields, making room for other whites to take their places. "Now the white man is different," he explains, removing another bottle from the closet. "Alright. Here's the top. He can fall over here in business," Gaither says, running his finger off the rim. "Fall over here in the hotel business, fall over here in teaching. . . . There are so many places for the white man to go to the top and so few places for the blacks to do anything. So the white man is not scuffling. Anytime you see a white man begging, he ain't no good. When I see them thumbing on the highway, you know what I say? 'You been free all your lives' and I step on the gas. Any white man in America that's begging—if he's not sick and has his mental faculties right—he just ain't no good. Any white man that can't make it in this country with all the opportunities that he's had, he just ain't no good. Now, I think that's responsible for our jealousy, for our envy—because there's not enough room at the top."

Will this ever change?

"Yes, sure it will. Look at the jobs opening up now. I go down to Eastern Airlines and I find my people selling tickets, stewards on airplanes. I go to the bank downtown and I see bank tellers. I go to the state capital building, and I see blacks sitting behind desks with secretaries. I see blacks in the legislature in Florida. Black mayors in Mississippi. You got blacks in Congress. You got black mayors in Gary, Indiana, Los Angeles, and Detroit. The more opportunity, the less of this will happen. Now, that doesn't make it right, but it's there. We just haven't had an opportunity to get recognition."

Few, if any, blacks will quarrel with Gaither's assertion that whites have always had more opportunities for advancement than blacks. But most blacks would probably take exception to his contention that they as a race have tended to "grab you and try to pull you back down." On the contrary, there have always been strong communal ties among blacks and, for the most part, they seem to have taken pride in seeing other members of their race advance; in spite of racial oppression, or maybe because of it, they have a collective sense of pride, a feeling that when one black succeeds, that's akin to a family member "making it." In the late 1950s and early 1960s, finding a black on TV, especially those in roles that projected any semblance of a positive image, was as difficult as trying to find a copy of *The Happy Hooker* in a Christian Science Reading Room. And when one did manage to slip through, parents would excitedly call their children into the room and afterwards neighbors would telephone each other, asking, "Did you see one of *us* on TV?" Football star O. J. Simpson, in an interview with *The New York Times,* alluded to the same reflected pride. "I was a black in the ghetto and Willie Mays gave me my pride," he said. "When he hit a home run, I was hitting it."

Perhaps the lack of consensus in the black community on Jake Gaither's contributions to social justice is inevitable. His reputation among whites was one of ready acceptance; this image was enhanced by Gaither's adroit use of the media. Jake has always received excellent press coverage—he sometimes brags that he has never had a "negative" story written or broadcast about him in Florida—because he is accessible, he has a listed telephone number, and he is what reporters call "good copy," full of an inexhaustible supply of epigrams and aphorisms.

C. J. Smith, III, former sports information director for

FAMU, says, "To writers, sports writers in particular, he's a natural for story material because he's cooperative and talkative, and always has a Texas-size crying towel in his hip pocket."

Aside from the discussion of whether Jake is an Uncle Tom, and ignoring the reams of favorable newspaper clippings, what is Jake Gaither really like away from the spotlight?

When assistant coaches and colleagues are asked what they least like in Gaither, they usually reply that it is his omnipresent quest for power and his penchant for flaunting his influence with whites. Almost everyone interviewed can recall that he has said at one time or another, "The urge for power is as great as the urge for sex."

This quest for power, the unending search for leverage and influence, is not unique to Jake Gaither. Lord Acton proclaimed that, "Power tends to corrupt and absolute power corrupts absolutely." Myra MacPherson's book *The Power Lovers: An Intimate Look at Politicians and Their Marriages* is an excellent, though unscientific, study of persons intoxicated with their own self-importance and a perpetual obsession to remain in power. Sometimes this can be taken to extremes as she notes in her book.

"There is one story of an ambitious Senator whose wife helped run his campaign," she writes. "One night, during a brief halt for lovemaking, her husband looked down at her and suddenly asked, 'How do you think we're doing in Brown County?'" The author adds, "The wife later divorced him and remarried his campaign manager, who presumably didn't care quite that much about Brown County."

Even Gaither's severest critics don't suggest that his problem is that serious, but they do agree that his never-ending lust for power is often overbearing.

"Jake and all of the old coaches are built out of the same mold," says a former assistant who is still on the FAMU staff. "They're all power hungry. He's very generous with his money—money doesn't interest him. It's the power."

D. C. Collington, another former sports information director under Gaither, says, "People who know him [Jake] don't like him. He'll always let you know that he can call Mr. Charlie and get what he wants."

Gaither has long been getting what he wants in Florida.

As early as 1954, a city park and recreation center in Tallahassee were named in his honor. In 1956, the lily-white Tallahassee Quarterback Club gave him its highest award. The state legislature, after the usual number of meaningless "whereases," passed a resolution in 1965 that, in part, reads:

"This Legislature requests the board of regents to name the new athletic center and gymnasium at the Florida Agricultural and Mechanical University in honor of Jake Gaither and to inscribe on the cornerstone of that building in an appropriate plaque setting forth some of the outstanding achievements and service which Jake Gaither has rendered to mankind."

Jake has even outmanuevered the president of Florida A&M on several occasions. For instance, one time he had persuaded the head of the appropriations committee in the state legislature to spearhead legislation that would give him more money for the athletic department. The money was sent directly to the president's office. Once the president made known his intention to divide the money among several other departments, Jake got on the telephone with some key legislators to inform them. They insisted that the money be spent exclusively on athletics, which it was.

Jake had once again prevailed.

Gaither's assistants say he always prevailed on the football field. Although Jake would delegate authority to his assistants, he still maintained the right to veto any decision, which is as it should be. But some say he disliked the idea of any coach disagreeing with him and tended to take such difference of opinions personally. Gaither felt everyone was entitled to their own opinion—as long as it agreed with his. The assistants say that Jake would try to charm them initially or use friendly persuasion. Once that failed, however, he would become pertinacious, refusing to budge and keeping everyone in the room until they capitulated.

"Jake wanted me to cut [dismiss] a boy because he had an Afro," says Athletic Director Tookes, who left the staff for several years. "The boy wanted to identify. I had an Afro; I wanted to identify. Hubbard [the present coach] has an Afro." He jokes, "Hubbard doesn't want a boy who doesn't have one."

Gaither is not unfamiliar with the criticism.

"This will make you understand me better than anything else," he says in reply. "There is nobody in the world who has had a better opportunity to know what is right and what is wrong; what is ethical or what is unethical than I have. My father was a minister, my mother was a schoolteacher. I learned to play cards in college—my peo-

ple wouldn't let me. I learned to dance in college—my
people were opposed to it. I never learned to play pool
because my father wouldn't let me go in a poolroom. My
people were very rigid on me, my father particularly. My
mother loved me so much that she wouldn't whip me like
my daddy would. I had a good home.

"Then I went to Knoxville College for eight years—four
years of high school and four years of college under God's
good people. And then I taught in church schools for eight
years. Then I worked in an Episcopal school for two years.
So *nobody* has had a better chance to know what's right
and what is wrong, what is ethical and what is unethical
than I have. I don't have to ask anybody to tell me. Ain't
no preacher in the pulpit can tell me anything that I don't
already know.

"Now, when I face an issue—fortunately my wife and
I think just alike in that aspect; if anything, she is more
inclined that way than I am. Every day that I did something that was wrong, I couldn't sleep at night because she
wouldn't let me sleep. Now, when an issue comes up and
I'm about to make a decision, I say, 'Is this the right thing
to do? Is this the ethical thing to do at this time?' When
I decide—I don't give a damn whether John Jones likes it
or not—I drive on. Now if he doesn't like me because I've
done what I think is right, the quicker I find out, the
better. His friendship ain't worth having anyway. If he
wants to dislike me because of my position that I take—
I don't want his friendship anyway. I haven't lost anything; I've just discovered something that I may not have
discovered. If my conscience is clear, I don't give a damn
whether he likes it or not. That's the way I operate."

Among coaches, the Jake Gaithers are the rule rather

than the exception when it comes to willingness to adapt. Many college coaches, who have been autocratic for decades, had to be towed into the twentieth century. Very few are as enlightened as Joe Paterno of Penn State, who says, "I don't think an athlete will buy this business that they'll do something just because you have 'coach' in front of your name. Football is a product of a culture and it's got to adapt to society; society isn't going to adapt to football."

Some of the crusty oldtimers, such as Bear Bryant, have softened, but not Gaither.

"A lot of these coaches say that you have to adjust yourself to these kids—you've got to relate to them," he snaps. "No, No. If he's got something that I admire, if he's got something very brilliant that I want to get, then I might adjust to him and then transfer to me some of his superior wisdom. But here's some little whippersnapper who is not dry behind the ears. Ain't had fifteen, sixteen, or seventeen years of experience, came right out of the backwoods or out of a house where they can't pay rent, where the daddy is a drunk and the mother is a whore, and he's gonna come up here and guide me. I get to him by adjusting myself to his standards? Ugh, ugh. He didn't come to college for me to get on his level. He came to college *hoping* to get on my level. Here's the way I look at it. I got the best football record of any coach in America—black, white, blue, or yellow. I didn't build that record by relating to him. I have learned over a period of forty-two years what gets results. Now, why should I let that little whippersnapper come up here and tell me how to run my business?"

What does Gaither say to players who want to wear an Afro?

"I say, 'Buddy, you take orders from me.' I don't take orders from him. I tell them I don't want it. If they ask why, I say, 'Because I don't like it.' I don't want any boy on the field who doesn't want to do what I want him to do. I don't want any boy on the field who doesn't want to please me. I'm not going to ask him to do what's wrong. It's the principle with me.

"I got sense enough to know that his long hair has nothing to do with his blocking or tackling. But if I can get him to cut his hair or beard off when he doesn't want to cut it, he's giving himself to me. He can give his heart to the Heart Fund, folks, but give me his butt. Then I can make him come to practice on time because he has surrendered to *me*. I can make him practice every day—he surrendered to *me*. I can make him drive when he's tired—he surrendered to *me*. He believes in *me*. Now, if I'm going to let him tell me what to do, he's going to lose his faith in me. So it's the principle of discipline to me. I don't want any boy on the field who doesn't want to do what I want him to do. And that's part of playing football. You got to pay the price.

"Do you think a kid likes to get up in this broiling sun and windsprint up and down the field? You think he does that because he wants to? No—he does it because I make him do it. I tell him to do it and he wants to please me and he does it. You think he throws himself across a man running at full speed because he loves that contact? Don't kid yourself. He does it because he expects the coach to say that's the way we expect him to play the game of football. I didn't pull a shotgun on him and make him come out. If he doesn't want to play under my rules, buddy, he can get the hell out of here. That's the only way a team is going to be coached.

"Now, the guy calling the shots got to be right. He's got to be straight. If you expect to be the leader, you can't go balling with him on Monday night and expect him to respect you on the field Tuesday. He can't see you drunk and whore-hopping around and take orders from you. He's got you then because he knows something on you that you don't want him to tell. If you're not willing to pay the price, get out of the field of coaching. When he respects you, you can call the shots to win. Now, that's how the game of football should be played. And don't tell me I'm wrong; I got a better record than anyone else."

Unfortunately, Gaither's obstinancy, his persistent criticism of football officials and Tennessee State's John Merritt, his lust for power, his arrogance, and his assuming the posture of a demigod cloud a more charitable side of Jake Gaither, the man.

For every Gaither detractor, there is at least one defender.

"He has had a great impact and he's in a class by himself," says Eddie Robinson of Grambling, the first black coach ever elected president of the American Football Coaches Association. "When you speak of the great coaches—people like Knute Rockne and [Frank] Leahy—you got to come on down and say Jake Gaither. You mention any of the great coaches and you have to mention Jake in the same sentence.

"This man has made an impact on the lives of boys he

coached, he has made an impact on the lives of people who met him—it's just something to meet the man. He has a double edge—he can cut it with what he has done in football and he's one of the greatest speakers of our time. He's one of the best men we've had in the profession."

Gaither has long been and remains an influential member of the AFCA; he is a permanent trustee.

Says Robinson, who was elected president in 1976, "I kind of feel that had Jake remained in football, he would have in time been the president of the American Football Coaches Association and he would have been before me. I feel that maybe I'm just carrying out something he started."

Even John Merritt of Tennessee State, Jake's nemesis, praises his contribution to the game.

"I certainly have utmost respect for him," Merritt says. "He did a lot for the game and for blacks. A lot of blacks criticized him for his relationship with whites. I think it was just like former black college presidents—some things had to be done that way for things to go on. This was the only way it could be done then, and had not someone done it like that, we wouldn't be where we are now. I think our greatest responsibility is to pick up where Jake left off. Next to Eddie Robinson, I'm the oldest black coach in a black school. I feel people like Jake, Mumford, Country Lewis, Taylor, Pop Long, and all of them did it the way they had to do it. I've got to do it a little bit better. I've got a bigger responsibility that led me to declare that I would never field a team where a black official was not present. We wouldn't play Notre Dame unless they had

some black officials on the field. Even though Jake didn't
do it that way, I think he probably did more to gain respect and admiration than any other coach of his era."

Jake has had a profound effect on hundreds of players
over the years.

"Jake Gaither is the greatest man in the world," says
Bob Hayes. "If I had to choose a father, Jake would be that
man. I mean that from my heart."

Purcell Houston, a former Florida A&M quarterback,
says, "Nobody is more inspirational. I'd follow him to hell
and back because of his beliefs. There is a part of him you
imitate to a degree."

Most of Jake's former players would probably say that
Larry Brown's assessment of the late Vince Lombardi
would also fit Jake. Brown said, "Coach Lombardi was a
teacher, the best I ever saw. But not just football. Coach
Lombardi taught me to be a man, to be proud of what I
am. He also taught me the wisdom of hard work and
dedication, and he proved to me that if you are better
prepared and more determined than the next man, you
will come out ahead of him. Even if he is more talented,
it will still hold true."

Jake Gaither is indeed a teacher, and he sounds like one
even when he's speaking.

"They say, 'Coach, you're old fashioned. You're
square,'" he says in his many lectures. " 'Don't you know
there is no such thing as right and wrong? What might be
right today may be wrong tomorrow. Right and wrong are
relative terms—they change.' Don't kid yourself. There
are certain eternal truths that never change. They were
true two thousand years ago and they'll be true two thou-

sand years hence: truth . . . honesty . . . integrity . . . loyalty
. . . humbleness . . . love thy father and thy mother . . .
decency. They never change—don't kid yourself. Do the
things that you know to be right and refuse to do the
things that you know to be wrong.

"I refer you to the Good Book. As you hope that people
will do unto you, do ye also unto them likewise. It's the
Golden Rule: Do unto others as you would have them do
unto you. That would solve every problem in the world
—the problem between capital and labor, the problem
between husband and wife, the problem between Jew
and Gentile, between black and white, and the problem
between nation and nation."

Although Gaither was a college professor and can at
times be professorial, his classroom was the football field.

"Often when a coach blows his whistle, indicating that
practice is over, the boys beg 'to run just one more play,' "
he wrote in his book, *The Split-Line T Offense.* "How
many times when the gong sounds at the end of a class
period does the English student beg for 'just one more
diagram' or the mathematician for just one more alge-
braic equation?"

Jake says football coaches have an advantage over other
teachers and even the players's parents.

"I've been a football coach for forty-two years," he says.
"I've had a chance to see the boy as no Mama or Papa ever
saw. I see that boy with his soul stripped naked. I can tell
you whether your son is a coward or a courageous man.
I can tell you whether your son is a liar and cheat or
whether he is an honest boy. I can tell whether your son
is a bigot or whether he has patience, tolerance, and un-

derstanding. I can tell you whether your son is an individualist or whether he will work in unity with other people. I can tell you whether your son will take orders and obey rules and regulations under which we live, or I can tell you whether he is a lawbreaker. We have a chance to see your son as nobody sees him. We see him with his soul stripped naked."

Gaither rubs his hair back, puffs on a cigarette, and looks a reporter directly in the eye as he says, "I find this: So many times youngsters *want* to be told. They'll go just as far as you'll let them. But they respond to reasoning. They know they're wrong, and if you approach them in the right way, they'll do right. Very few of them—when you really pin them down—will say, 'I'm right, you're wrong.' "

The Gaithers have no children; they lost a son prematurely. But they have not been without children, for they have adopted every player on each team, many of whom ran by the house to sample Mrs. Gaither's cooking or discuss a personal problem with Jake. Most of the players have come from families in two income brackets—low income and high outgo. They grew up in what some sociologists describe as "broken homes," which is a misnomer. It is the persons inside the house, not the structure itself, who are broke. When freshmen players arrive each year the first thing Gaither tells them is, "Boys, you come to me when you're in trouble, when someone in your family is sick, when you need help in the classroom. You come to me."

And when the players ran into difficulties, Jake assisted them, whether in arranging a class schedule or in solving a financial problem. Jake often used his personal funds to help a student remain in school. Unlike many of the major schools, Florida A&M had neither the money nor the inclination to slip athletes money under the table, if there was indeed a table at all. Consequently it was a continuing struggle to keep players in school, even the ones on scholarship.

Even so, Jake has remained above reproach in his recruiting and handling of finances. There has never been a scintilla of evidence or even a suggestion that Gaither has misappropriated funds or done anything unethical in his coaching career.

"With his great record and all, he has never agreed to win at any cost," says Pete Griffin, his longtime assistant. "Jake has always been ethical, and he has never done anything to win that was not in the rule book or in the Christian spirit."

Although there were only limited scholarship funds, Gaither saw them not only as an opportunity to acquire outstanding athletes, but as a chance to provide a player an opportunity to get the college education that he had not even thought about.

"I can remember hundreds and hundreds of kids who have been inspired to get a college education who otherwise would have never had a chance," he says. "Now that's why I'm against those inferior white colleges that don't give enough scholarships. Think of all the boys they could influence. Suppose little Bobby Hayes hadn't been given a scholarship. His daddy was a paraplegic and his mother a domestic; that boy would have never gotten to college. Denson sat here last night and said he doesn't know his mother or father—his grandmother raised him. That boy probably would have never seen the inside of a college. Smith's [not his real name] daddy is an alcoholic. He came off a farm and would not have gotten to college without a scholarship. Not only did he get a scholarship, but I took his brother."

Jake says Florida A&M is also turning away too many needy applicants. After losing to Tennessee State 45–6 in 1965, he chose to use the game's aftermath to lament the rising academic standards. He said that if Bob Hayes, Willie Galimore, and Althea Gibson—all FAMU graduates—were applying to Florida A&M today, they would not be accepted.

"People like those certainly helped our school, and they've turned out to be good citizens," Gaither said. "But with the rigid rules we've got here now, none of them could get in school.

"My people aren't supermen. The black can't overcome one hundred years overnight. They've been hungry all their lives. They've been deprived. Their fathers didn't go to college. Our boys don't come from wealthy families who have come to Florida to live. The bulk of our boys come out of the woods. The boy's father is a truck driver and his mother is a domestic. It'll be forty or fifty years before this changes. So measuring up to the white college entrance examinations has to be a gradual process.

"I can't get the best boys out of our state anymore. I can recruit them, but I can't get them into school. The days of the great teams here are over. If they want Ivy League standards here, they're going to have to settle for Ivy League football."

Those players Jake did manage to get, he followed both on and off-field. Bob Hayes gives an example.

"I was in a New York meet and pulled a leg muscle," Hayes recalls. "I called Coach long-distance and he sent George [George Thompson, the athletic trainer] to town, the AAU doctor, and jumped on a flight to New York himself. I told him, 'Why don't you go on back home? I'm doing fine—I can take care of myself.' Coach told me, 'You don't leave a nineteen-year-old boy in New York City who says he can take care of himself.'

"I was training down in Miami and Coach called to see if my leg was alright. I told him it was and that I needed some money. He sent it and I flew to L.A. I won the meet and he flew all the way to California, shook my hand, and headed right back to Tallahassee."

And there was also the case of another Florida A&M alumnus, Althea Gibson, the first black to win tennis championships at Wimbledon and Forest Hills, as well as the first black to represent the United States in the Wightman Cup competition. Althea, now the athletic commissioner of New Jersey, played tennis and basketball at Florida A&M on scholarship.

"I remember many afternoons when she would come into my office and argue about quitting school," says Gaither, who was then athletic director and head of the department of health and physical education. "She'd wind up running out into the hall and slamming the door. Then she would come back and say, 'Pop, are you mad with me?' 'No, honey,' I'd always tell her. 'I'm not mad with you.' She needed understanding."

Gaither's understanding, generosity, and concern was

not limited to his football players or physical education majors.

For example, during a break between sessions of his 1971 coaching clinic, he stopped to speak to another student in the school's gymnasium. After extending his hand, Jake said, "Don't give me a limp handshake," in a firm, but comforting tone. "Can't you grip my hand like I grip yours?" The student replied, "Yes, sir," and squeezed Jake's hand. Gaither, in turn, said, "Now, that's more like it." As he and a reporter continued to walk down the hall, he said, "I want all of our students to be ready to step out in the world whether they are football players or not. They can't be giving anyone a limp handshake."

Those who are around Gaither say the incident in the hallway was not out of the ordinary; Jake does things like that all the time.

And he has given more than just advice, he has also given his money.

He has given it to students and faculty. Several persons still owe him money, including one man who defaulted on a $900 loan Jake co-signed. Yet he continued to give freely of what funds he had.

One staff member who had worked in the athletic department approached Gaither several years ago about co-signing a loan. The young man explained his reason for wanting the money and Gaither said, "Go to the bank and tell them I said it's okay." The man paused, hoping that Jake would specify which bank. After no answer, he politely asked, "Which bank, Coach?" Jake replied, "Hell, any of them." The staff member hurried downtown—to the bank of his choice—and sure enough, the manager told him all he needed was Gaither's signature.

Perhaps Gaither's greatest contribution, even more than money, has been the deep and lasting influence he has had on hundreds of young men who came under his guidance. Many have since become oustanding professional football players, but even more have distinguished themselves in law, medicine, education, science, and government service. Jake was able to instill in them what he calls "the Spirit of Excellence," the drive to excel in every endeavor rather than offer excuses. That gift is priceless.

"Excuses are no good," he always advised them. "Your friends don't need them and your enemies won't believe them. So why make them?"

Jake taught his players that there is no substitute for hard work and that, although one faces obstacles in life, through hard work and determination one can still come out on top. To illustrate his point he repeats a story told to him by the president of Knoxville College.

"In the mountains of Kentucky," he says, "farmers used to grow their crops around the mountainside. They used to bring produce into Middlesboro, Kentucky, and sell it to vendors; the farmers would bring beans, tomatoes, corn, and potatoes.

"About three o'clock in the morning, Farmer Jones saw a light in the smokehouse of Farmer Brown. So Farmer Jones walked across to Farmer Brown's place and said, 'What are you doing, Farmer Brown?' Brown said, 'I'm loading up a wagon full of potatoes. I'm going to take them into town and sell them.' He was shoveling potatoes onto his wagon bed. Farmer Brown said, 'I noticed you got some big potatoes there and some little ones. Why don't you put the little ones on the bottom and the big ones on the top—it'll present a better picture and you'll sell more potatoes.'

"Old Farmer Brown stopped shoveling, turned around and looked at him. He said, 'I've been hauling potatoes to town the past fifteen or twenty years and the road was long and rough. But I found this: If the road is long enough, if the road is rocky enough, the big potato will come to the top and the little potato will go the the bottom.' "

Jake repeats the last sentence slowly, for emphasis: "If the road is long enough, if the road is rocky enough, the big potato will come to the top and the little potato will go to the bottom."

Obviously Jake Gaither is a big potato.

13

Lights Out

At 7:03 P.M. Eastern Daylight Time on September 20, 1975, Alonzo Smith Gaither eased behind the steering wheel of his Lincoln Continental to begin a five-minute drive to Florida A&M's Bragg Memorial Stadium, where the Rattlers were playing their season opener against Albany State College. Almost simultaneously a visiting reporter crawled into the back seat of the automobile and Mrs. Sadie Gaither, a plump, cheerful woman, slid next to her husband in the front seat, closing the door behind her. Gaither slowly backed down the long, steep drive that leads up to his house.

The Gaithers and their guest were on their way to see a football game. Moments earlier, Jake had been standing in his trophy room discussing his career with the reporter —and reviewing the more than 100 awards that grace the room.

A photo hangs on one wall with the inscription, "To Jake Gaither, with great respect and admiration from his fellow coach and friend—Darrell Royal." A picture of Claude Kirk, the former segregationist governor of Florida, is signed: "Put me in, Coach, I'm ready. Best Regards to one of the all-time greats—Claude Kirk."

A large plaque honoring Gaither as Small College Coach of the Year (1962) hangs on the room's east wall. A few feet away, hangs another plaque, commemorating his induction into the Tennessee Hall of Fame. There is also a trophy from the Touchdown Club of Washington, D.C., awarded to him in 1969 for "Outstanding Contribution to Football." Perched in a silver bowl is a football given to Gaither by Willie Galimore denoting the Chicago Bears' 1963 Western Division Championship.

Across the room is an engraved reprint of a newspaper article about Gaither. Quoted in the story is a poem entitled "A Tribute to Jake," written by Purcell Houston, a FAMU quarterback in the early 1950s. It reads:

Your faith in God and devotion to mankind
Shall write your name on the sands of time,
The archive shall reveal and the bells shall ring
About a football coach great enough to walk with Kings.

There are dozens of other awards—a key to the city of Tampa; Distinguished Citizen of Middlesboro, Kentucky; Ambassador of Good Will for the city of Chattanooga, Tennessee; a plaque noting his induction into the Helms Foundation Hall of Fame; pictures of Lyndon Johnson, Hubert Humphrey, former governors, celebrities, and past teams.

But the awards that catches the eye immediately are in a tall cabinet near the room's rear entrance. Stored in the wood and glass cabinet is recognition for winning The Big Three, or what some call the Coaches Triple Crown—the Amos Alonzo Stagg Award, the Walter Camp Award, and membership in the National Football Foundation Hall of Fame.

More than six years have passed since Gaither's retirement was announced by A&M President Benjamin L. Perry, Jr., at a press conference January 20, 1970.

Many of the reporters questions then were addressed to Jake. He said, "My wife and I talked it over and she wants me to quit. My brothers and I talked it over and they want me to quit. The reason is simply this: I didn't want to press my luck too long. Since being a coach at Florida A&M, I have survived a brain operation, I have survived blindness, and I have survived a broken leg. The Old Man upstairs has been mighty good to Jake."

He added later, "They talk about what I have given football. No, it's the opposite, it's what football has given me. I can never repay the game of football for the fine things that football has been to me. I got a few more years, and I want to spend them doing whatever I can for the good of the university."

Gaither's reference to having "a few more years" was one of the few times he has alluded to death. He was born April 11, 1903, in Dayton, Tennessee, but he has refused to give his age during his later years and has almost never discussed the subject of death.

"Just say that I am sixty-five, because somebody has already printed that I was," he told a reporter in the late 1960s. "Say also that I'm gonna stay sixty-five for a long time. Say that I feel as good as I did a dozen years ago, and in some ways better . . . physically better, mentally about the same."

This author asked him in September 1975: Having lived

such a full life, do you ever think about death?

"I don't want to think about it," he replied. "The hardest thing in the world for me to do was to make a will. My wife and I finally decided how crazy that was. But I didn't want to think about it. A guy came here wanting to sell me a plot. You know that guy was trying to sell cemetery plots," Gaither said, his voice uncharacteristically high. "I said, 'Man, get the hell out of here.' I said, 'I don't want you to talk to me about dying. I ain't planning for that.' I practically had to drive him out of the house. And he just insisted—kind of like an undertaker, you know. I said, 'Hell, I don't want to think about that.' Of course, I try to live decently. I'm not a religious fanatic, but I'm a very strong supporter of the church. Life has been good to Jake."

Whether we like it or not, death will come to all of us. And how does Gaither want to be remembered?

"Oh, I'd like to be remembered as honest, frank, courageous, humble, kind-hearted, an individual who feels that the higher you got—the more honors you attain, the more prestige you build—the more humble you should become, because God has been good to you. I believe that. I see people rise, get wealthy and powerful positions, and they start kicking people around. I think when you're lucky enough to get those things, you should be more concerned about helping other people, because God has been good to you.

"I still haven't answered your question . . . a square shooter who's concerned about the welfare of others. I want to be fair in dealing with people and always sensitive to the needs of others."

Upon reaching the state's mandatory retirement age of seventy in 1973, Gaither retired from Florida A&M. He earns more money now speaking across the country than he did when he was coaching. And although he is not coaching anymore, he remains one of Florida's most recognizable figures, to both blacks and whites. His audiences accord him standing ovations almost everywhere he appears. He is frequently stopped on the street, as was the case the night he was driving to the FAMU football game.

As Gaither's automobile came within a mile of the stadium, a black teen-ager yelled, "Hi, Jake." Turning to his friends, the boy said excitedly, "Here's Jake." Each of them, about seven in all, spoke to the former coach. Gaither grinned broadly, rolled down his window and replied, "Hi, baby," his voice barely audible. "Howya doing?" As the car inched forward, Mrs. Gaither said softly, "They used to call you Coach, now they just say Jake." Gaither agreed, saying, "Yeah, I know."

About a block from the stadium, the traffic began piling up, with most cars bumper-to-bumper. Jake waited patiently, returning the waves and pleasantries to the many that acknowledged his presence. Finally the car came to a point about forty yards from the stadium. The traffic officer had been directing everyone to the parking lot to the right. When Gaither's turn came, the uniformed officer nodded and waved him to a passageway to the left, which led directly into the stadium. When the car behind Gaither attempted to follow him, the policeman put up his right hand, signaling the driver to halt, and then directed him to the parking lot to the right.

With synchronized precision, two security men opened the stadium gates upon recognizing Gaither. Jake drove his car into the stadium, speaking to the guards along the way. There was only one other vehicle parked in the stadium at the time, an ambulance parked on the visitors' side of the field. Jake drove around the asphalt track that encircles the field and parked directly in front of the ambulance, the rear of his car awkwardly protruding toward the field.

Gaither, accompanied by his wife and the reporter, began the climb the long flight of steps leading to the press box, where Roosevelt Wilson, the school's sports information director, had reserved three seats for them. (The silver-haired Gaither walks with a noticeable limp, a result of his trick knee as a player at Knoxville College and having his leg broken in 1967 during the football game against Southern University.)

The discussion in the press box was, as it was throughout the stadium before the kick-off: Can the Rattlers come back?

FAMU had gone through a five-year slump, beginning with Jake's retirement. Some of Gaither's more cynical critics contend it was designed that way, to make Jake's impressive record appear even greater by comparison, a charge that Gaither dismisses as utter nonsense.

Whatever the merits of the argument, there can be no dispute as to what happened on the football field. From 1937, the year Gaither joined Head Coach Bill Bell and his brother, Horace, at Florida A&M, through 1969, the year Jake retired, FAMU had won 252 games and lost 46, an average of less than two losses each season. But in the first four years that Gaither was out of the coaching ranks, FAMU lost 22 games, an average of 5.5 losses a season, while winning only 21.

Upon Jake's retirement, Pete Griffin, who had worked in tandem with Gaither for a quarter of a century, was promoted to head coach. In his twenty-six years as top assistant and defensive coordinator under Gaither, FAMU allowed only 2,635 points in 235 games, an average of 10.4 points per game. In Pete's first year as head coach, FAMU won 5 and lost 5, with opponents averaging 19.4 points a game. Griffin retired after one season.

Clarence Montgomery, a former FAMU honorable mention All-America end and head coach of Tallahassee's Lincoln High School [his record there was 79 wins, 23 losses, and 10 ties], was chosen to take over for the 1971 season. Montgomery died late in the season, and the team finished the season with 6 wins and 5 losses. Gaither, still athletic director, turned to another of his former pupils, this time selecting James J. Wilson, the quarterback of FAMU's perfect (9–0) season in 1942. After two seasons, Williams had accumulated a record of 10 wins, 12 losses, and his walking papers.

Then for the first time since Jake Gaither was hired in 1945, Florida A&M went outside its ranks for a coach. Up to that point, even all of the assistant coaches had been A&M graduates. The job was given to Rudy Hubbard, a former running back and coach under Woody Hayes at Ohio State. Hubbard was respected for his football knowledge and his recruiting skills, having personally recruited two-time Heisman Trophy winner Archie Griffin, Quarterback Cornelius Greene and Lineman John Hicks.

When Hubbard took over in 1974, FAMU fans expected him to be Moses—the one who would lead them to the Promised Land, or if not to the Promised Land, at least back to where Gaither had taken them. Evidently Hubbard thought he knew his way out of the wilderness, too. Upon accepting the job, he immediately contracted a severe case of foot-in-mouth disease, vowing to "win them all." His record that year? Six wins and 5 losses.

Understandably, Rattlers fans were eager to see what Hubbard's second season would bring. All week they had been chanting, "The Rattlers are back." But the game against Albany State would prove whether the Rattlers were indeed back, or were just green snakes masquerading as Rattlers.

Throughout the pregame warm-up, Gaither munched on peanuts, something he had refused to do on the day of a game for more than three decades, supposedly because they brought bad luck. He also refused to eat any food that contained peanuts. The only other superstition he had was wearing an old faded jacket when he was coaching at Henderson Institute in North Carolina.

But this was now Hubbard's game, not Jake's.

In the opening minutes of the game, FAMU played as though they were definitely back, scoring touchdowns in their first two possessions and taking a 14–0 lead. FAMU scored again early in the second quarter on a 29-yard field goal to increase its lead by 3 points. Albany State and FAMU each scored a touchdown, and the halftime score was FAMU 23, Albany 7. Before the game was over the Rattlers added a field goal in the third quarter and scored 28 points in the fourth quarter. The final score was 54–7, the most points FAMU had scored since 1969. (The team finished the season with 8 wins and 2 losses.)

"Y-e-a-h! Those boys looked like somethin' out there tonight," Gaither said afterward. "I ain't seen that kind of ball since 1969," an allusion to his final year.

Jake invited Mrs. Lillian W. Higgins, his former secretary, and Mrs. Kathy Wilson, wife of the sports publicist, to stop by the house later, and both accepted the invitation.

The trip home took about ten minutes. Gaither took a circuitous route back, trying to avoid the line of automobiles and horde of jubilant students.

At last the Lincoln Continental turned into the driveway. It was a long and slow pull—the foot of the driveway is particularly steep, and when a car traverses it, the vehicle seems almost perpendicular to the ground. When the climb was over, Jake put the car in "park," turned off the ignition and went inside with his wife and the visiting reporter.

The house, unlike in the days when Jake was coaching, was frighteningly quiet.

In the old days, streams of students, faculty, and alumni would meet faithfully at the Gaithers' after each home game, usually to bask in victory, replay the night's game, and tell jokes, especially about Gaither.

Purcell "Nick" Houston, a jocular former quarterback and later athletic director of Blanche Ely High School in Pompano Beach, Florida, until it fell foe to the city's desegregation efforts, can mimic Gaither perhaps better than anyone else. He has held court at many of those after-game parties.

Houston invariably would tell the story about the time that he first went to Florida A&M too poor even to pay attention. He said once that his family had exhausted their money and, if he hadn't gotten financial aid from the school, he would have been forced to withdraw.

"I didn't have a dime and I didn't know where I was going to get any money," Houston says. "So I went to see Jake, told him my problem, and waited for an answer. After a few seconds he got up out of his chair, tapped on his wallet, and said, 'Hell, what do you think I'm sitting on —Fort Knox?' "

Houston says Gaither arranged for him to obtain a student loan, but with all the laughter—partly because of the joke and partly at the way Houston imitates Gaither—the crowd would usually miss the last part of the story.

Houston also tells about the time that Jake, who insists that his assistants be circumspect in both their public and private lives, was supposed to have gotten word that one of his assistant coaches had engaged in sexual intercourse with a FAMU student. The story is obviously apocryphal, but that does not dampen Purcell's enthusiasm.

"I understand that one of you boys has been sleeping with one of the girls," Gaither is supposed to have said after summoning his assistant coaches.

"Now, you know we must be above reproach at all times. We're supposed to be teaching these kids how to live clean, upright, Christian lives, and one of you has been out there wallowing in the gutter. When I find out who did it, I'm going to fire him.

"This young lady has been bragging all over campus about how she has slept with one of my coaches. It's a disgrace for something to happen like this after all this work I've put into building this program. We have the best small college football program in the nation, and now one of you is destroying everything we've built after years and years of hard work."

Jake shook his head at that point, pondering the impact of the indiscretion.

"Fortunately, we have something to go on in this case," Gaither remarked. "The girl still has the coach's cap, and by the process of elimination we can find out who the guilty party is."

The coaches who could account for their cap gave a collective sigh of relief.

Jake continued.

"Pete," he asked, "Where is your cap?"

Griffin replied, "Here it is, Coach," waving the orange and green cap.

Gaither went down the line.

"Where is yours, Tookes?"

Tookes responded, "Right here, Coach," flashing it before Gaither's eyes.

"Oglesby?"

"Here it is, Coach."

"Kittles, where's yours?"

"Here," he said, taking it out of a pocket.

"Mungen, can you account for yours?"

"Yes, here it is," came the reply.

"B-o-b-b-y L-a-n-g. You're the last one," Jake said, almost accusingly. "Baby, can you show me your cap?"

Lang produced his and Gaither was suddenly bemused, scratching his head and staring at the floor.

Finally one of the coaches asked, "Coach, where is yours?"

Gaither, unable to locate it, searched each pocket frantically, began stammering, and then yelled, "Everybody get out of here."

As Purcell finished embellishing each sentence, his audience rolled in laughter.

Another former player would tell about the first time that Jake met Shorty Shannon, his athletic trainer, back in the 1950s. They say that Shannon, who stands a shade under five feet with platform shoes on, entered Gaither's office one day. Jake, who didn't see him enter, said, "Baby, get off of your knees. You don't have to bow down to Coach."

Assistant coaches tell about another time when Jake was leading the team in prayer before a game. They say Gaither was in fine form that night: "O Merciful Lord, we are before Thee again tonight in need of Your generous blessings. You have been good to us so far this season—*somebody turn that damn radio off*—excuse me, Lord . . . We do not ask for victory, but only that we be allowed to do Your will."

Gaither loved the banter, usually joining in himself.

He recalls the time President George W. Gore, Jr., in an appeal to the state legislature for additional funding, said, "We want to have a university that our football team can be proud of."

Invariably, someone mentioned the Christmas season when the following letter appeared in the local newspaper: "Please, Santa, bring FSU a football team, and A&M an opponent."

Purcell says that Gaither once woke his team up at about 3:00 A.M. two days before an important game. He says Gaither told his groggy players, "Kids, I had a dream that we forgot our new defense for this game, and I want to go over it one more time."

That's the way the Gaither household roared after the games in the Good Ol' Days.

September 20, 1975, was a game night, yet no one would have known it by visiting the Gaither home.

When Jake returned home, he first flicked on the TV in the living room to learn the day's football scores. Moments later, he walked back to the trophy room with the reporter. The only other people in the trophy room or the house that night were Sadie; Kathy Wilson, wife of the sports information director, and the Wilson children. Jake's former secretary had come by for several minutes, but left.

Roosevelt Wilson, the sports publicist, came by about 11:30. He and Jake discussed the night's game and at about midnight, Wilson, his family, and the reporter departed, leaving only Jake and Sadie. After they left, the lights in the Gaither home were dimmed. Maybe it was a symbolic gesture, considering that the lights on Gaither's coaching days were also dimmed.

Gone were the days of Power and Glory.

Appendix

PARTIAL LIST OF HONORS AWARDED TO JAKE GAITHER

1953 Pigskin Club of Washington, D.C., Award

1954 City of Tallahassee names recreation center, park, and golf course in Gaither's honor

1956 Receives Tallahassee Quarterback Club's Service Award

1960 Named Coach of the Decade by the 100 Percent Wrong Club of Atlanta, Georgia.

1961 Associated Press names Gaither small college Coach of the Year

Inducted into the Helms Foundation Football Hall of Fame

1962 Elected small college Coach of the Year by the American Football Coaches Association

Inducted into the Florida Sports Writers Hall of Fame

1963 Inducted into the Knoxville College Hall of Fame

Receives award from the Football Writers Association of America

Writes book titled *The Split-Line T Offense*

1965 Florida legislature votes to name new structure at Florida A&M The Jake Gaither Athletic Center and Gymnasium

1969 The Touchdown Club of Washington, D.C., gives award to Gaither for "The Outstanding Contribution to Football in the Nation"

Named permanent trustee of the American Football Coaches Association

Named National Association of Intercollegiate Athletics (NAIA) Coach of the Year

1975 Winner of three highest awards given to a coach, becoming the first person to win all three in the same year (he won all three in month of January). The awards were the Alonzo Stagg Award, which is voted by member coaches of the American Football Coaches Association; the Walter Camp Award, presented by the Walter Camp Foundation at Yale to the person who has made outstanding contributions to athletics and humanity; and induction into the National Football Foundation's Hall of Fame. Selected member of Orange Bowl Committee

1976 Receives Florida A&M "Merit of Achievement Award"

JAKE GAITHER'S COACHING RECORD
AT FLORIDA A&M (1945–1969)

1945 (9–1–0)

A&M	Opponent	Opp. Score
17	Alabama State	2
39	Morris Brown	0
25	Knoxville	0
54	Tuskegee Institute	20
24	Clark	19
46	Morehouse	6
26	Wilberforce	20
33	Louisiana Normal	12
20	Tennessee State	18
6	Wiley (OBC)	32
290		129

1946 (6–4–1)

A&M	Opponent	Opp. Score
35	Alabama State	0
32	Clark	0
21	Tuskegee Institute	12
7	Morris Brown	0
19	Southern University	38
6	Kentucky State	13
27	Knoxville	0
14	Wilberforce	22
18	Fisk	0
14	Lincoln (Pa.)	20
0	Wiley (OBC)	6
193		111

1947 (9–1–0)

A&M	Opponent	Opp. Score
58	Alabama State	12
33	Clark	6
19	Tuskegee Institute	6
6	Morris Brown	0
13	Southern	9
14	Kentucky State	12
26	Knoxville	0
0	Shaw	19
6	Bethune-Cookman	0
7	Hampton Institute (OBC)	0
182		64

1948 (8–2–0)

A&M	Opponent	Opp. Score
41	Alabama State	0
20	Benedict	6
39	Tuskegee Institute	0
13	Morris Brown	6
23	Kentucky State	14
7	Shaw	6
26	Xavier (La.)	6
36	Clark	12
12	Southern University	32
0	Virginia Union (OBC)	19
217		101

1949 (7–2–0)

A&M	Opponent	Opp. Score
58	Tuskegee Institute	0
31	Morris Brown	20
13	Southern University	31
58	Xavier (La.)	13
55	Alcorn	7
39	Ft. Valley State	0
34	Allen Univ.	0
13	Benedict	0
14	North Carolina A&T (OBC)	20
315		91

1950 (7–1–1)

A&M	Opponent	Opp. Score
20	Benedict	13
26	Tuskegee Institute	0
20	Morris Brown	0
14	North Carolina A&T	9
26	Texas College	6
33	Bethune-Cookman	7
40	Allen	13
0	Southern University	0
6	Central State (OBC)	13
185		61

1951 (7–1–1)

54	Benedict	0
13	Morris Brown	20
7	North Carolina A&T	7
48	Texas College	13
26	Bethune-Cookman	13
34	Allen	0
36	Southern University	6
48	Ft. Valley State	0
67	North Carolina College (OBC)	6
333		65

1952 (8–2–0)

41	Benedict	7
27	Morris Brown	7
19	North Carolina A&T	12
48	Texas College	13
7	Bethune-Cookman	8
45	Allen	7
51	Ft. Valley State	0
10	Prairie View	7
13	Southern University	25
27	Virginia State (OBC)	7
288		93

1953 (10–1–0)

33	Texas College	0
45	Benedict	0
31	Ft. Valley State	0
8	Tyndall A.F. Base	0
20	Morris Brown	0
65	Xavier (La.)	0
39	Bethune-Cookman	7
33	North Carolina A&T	13
28	Allen	10
33	Southern University	25
27	Prairie View (OBC)	33
362		88

1954 (8–1–0)

39	Texas College	14
36	Benedict	6
27	Morris Brown	7
19	Prairie View	7
25	Xavier (La.)	7
14	North Carolina A&T	7
68	Allen	13
20	Southern University	59
67	Maryland State (OBC)	19
315		139

1955 (7–1–1)

A&M	Opponent	Opp. Score
80	Benedict	6
49	Ft. Valley State	0
14	Morris Brown	6
32	Bethune-Cookman	0
60	Xavier	19
28	North Carolina A&T	28
34	Allen	7
51	Southern University	0
21	Grambling (OBC)	28
369		94

1956 (8–1–0)

A&M	Opponent	Opp. Score
25	North Carolina College	0
33	Ft. Valley State	6
46	Morris Brown	14
54	Bethune-Cookman	6
68	Xavier (La.)	6
49	North Carolina A&T	13
58	Allen	6
34	Southern University	6
39	Tennessee State (OBC)	41
406		98

1957 (9–0–0)

74	Ft. Valley State	0
27	Morris Brown	0
45	Bethune-Cookman	6
40	Benedict	2
42	North Carolina A&T	6
42	Allen	0
32	Southern University	6
14	North Carolina College	0
27	Maryland State (OBC)	21
343		41

1958 (7–2–0)

68	Benedict	0
13	Morris Brown	12
29	Bethune-Cookman	0
28	South Carolina State	8
37	North Carolina A&T	22
52	Allen	14
6	Southern University	35
22	Texas Southern	18
8	Prairie View (OBC)	26
263		135

1959 (10–0–0)

74	Benedict	0
64	Wiley	0
6	Morris Brown	0
68	Bethune-Cookman	6
34	South Carolina State	12
28	North Carolina A&T	16
52	Allen	8
21	Southern University	14
36	Texas Southern	8
28	Prairie View (OBC)	7
411		71

1960 (9–1–0)

68	Benedict	0
46	Lincoln (Mo.)	6
64	Morris Brown	0
97	Bethune-Cookman	0
80	South Carolina State	0
49	North Carolina A&T	19
35	Allen	0
6	Southern University	14
30	Texas Southern	8
40	Langston (OBC)	26
515		73

1961 (10–0–0)

A&M	Opponent	Opp. Score
52	Benedict	0
49	Lincoln (Mo.)	6
56	Morris Brown	0
76	Bethune-Cookman	0
60	South Carolina State	0
34	North Carolina A&T	12
71	Allen	0
46	Southern University	0
48	Texas Southern	7
14	Jackson State (OBC)	8
506		33

1962 (9–1–0)

A&M	Opponent	Opp. Score
60	Benedict	0
52	Lincoln (Mo.)	6
36	Morris Brown	12
52	Bethune-Cookman	6
20	Tennessee State	0
38	North Carolina A&T	6
67	Allen	0
25	Southern University	0
48	Texas Southern	18
6	Jackson State (OBC)	22
404		70

1963 (8–2–0)

A&M	Opponent	Opp. Score
44	Lincoln (Mo.)	6
14	Benedict	0
66	Morris Brown	0
12	Tennessee State	14
54	Central State	0
32	North Carolina A&T	0
37	Southern University	0
38	Bethune-Cookman	14
14	Texas Southern	20
30	Morgan State (OBC)	7
341		61

1964 (9–1–0)

A&M	Opponent	Opp. Score
14	Lincoln (Mo.)	3
56	Central State	15
28	Morris Brown	0
22	Tennessee State	20
54	Benedict	6
46	North Carolina A&T	24
20	Southern University	43
31	Bethune-Cookman	14
24	Texas Southern	14
42	Grambling (OBC)	15
337		154

1965 (7–3–0)

A&M	Opponent	Opp. Score
25	Allen	12
19	South Carolina State	13
28	Alabama A&M	14
23	Morris Brown	7
6	Tennessee State	45
28	North Carolina A&T	14
41	Southern University	38
47	Bethune-Cookman	8
21	Texas Southern	34
7	Morgan State	36
245		221

1966 (7–3–0)

A&M	Opponent	Opp. Score
43	Allen	3
3	South Carolina State	8
56	Benedict	12
22	Morris Brown	15
0	Tennessee State	29
64	North Carolina A&T	18
13	Southern University	17
37	Bethune-Cookman	13
41	Texas Southern	12
43	Alabama A&M (OBC)	26
322		153

1967 (8–2–0)

A&M	Opponent	Opp. Score
43	Allen	0
25	South Carolina State	0
45	Alabama A&M	36
44	Morris Brown	0
8	Tennessee State	32
63	North Carolina A&T	6
36	Southern University	25
30	Bethune-Cookman	6
30	Texas Southern	6
25	Grambling (OBC)	28
349		139

1968 (8–2–0)

A&M	Opponent	Opp. Score
48	Allen	0
25	South Carolina State	3
33	Alabama A&M	7
7	Morris Brown	0
32	Tennessee State	13
6	North Carolina A&T	9
33	Southern University	25
23	Bethune-Cookman	20
20	Texas Southern	7
9	Alcorn (OBC)	36
236		120

1969 (8–1–0)

27	South Carolina State	7
42	Alabama A&M	14
45	Morris Brown	15
20	Tennessee State	33
26	North Carolina A&T	9
10	Southern University	7
60	Bethune-Cookman	15
34	Tampa	28
23	Grambling (OBC)	19
287		147

Jake Gaither retired with a record of 203 wins, 36 losses, and 4 ties.